"*Work It* is THE likeable guide to business and personal success for women at any stage of their careers."   —Gail Galuppo, CMO, Aflac

". . . great, practical advice about how to succeed in business and in life, told through the stories of many impressive women."
                              —Lauren Hobart, president, DICK'S Sporting Goods

"Keep *Work It* in your bag and pull it out anytime you need a nugget of inspiration from any one of these amazing women! This is a great and essential read."
                              —Betty Liu, founder, Radiate, Inc., and
                              anchor, Bloomberg Television

"This is like having fifty brilliant women in your corner, guiding you along your path to success."
                              —Telisa Yancy, CMO, American Family Insurance, 2016
                              Ebony Power 100, and 2017 *AdAge* Woman to Watch

"*Work It* is a must-read for any woman, whatever she's doing and whatever her ambition. Carrie Kerpen combines fascinating, frank stories from women who've faced all sorts of challenges and overcome them, with her own searingly honest account of the ups and downs, missteps and landings that got her to her own success. This is the female equivalent of Ben Horowitz's *The Hard Thing About Hard Things*—Carrie and her riveting interviewees tell it like it really is, to arm you with hardheaded advice to achieve your own dreams."
                              —Cindy Gallop, founder, MakeLoveNotPorn

"What I like so much about [*Work It*] is its deliberate accessibility. *Work It* will speak to those of you who aren't feeling the #Girlboss or "lean in" or "badass" bause personas that so many books tout currently. Still, the 'secrets' that make up the book still originate from some of the most successful or powerful women in business, including Kerpen herself."
                              —800 CEO Read, "Fall Favorites by and for Feminists"

"[*Work It*] will resonate with those currently struggling to achieve their goals in the business world and will encourage them to keep going."
                              —*Publishers Weekly*

WORK *IT*

WORK *IT*

Secrets for Success from
the **BOLDEST** Women
in Business

CARRIE KERPEN

A TarcherPerigee Book

tarcherperigee

An imprint of Penguin Random House LLC
375 Hudson Street
New York, New York 10014

Most TarcherPerigee books are available at special quantity discounts
for bulk purchase for sales promotions, premiums, fund-raising, and
educational needs. Special books or book excerpts also can
be created to fit specific needs. For details, write:
SpecialMarkets@penguinrandomhouse.com.

Library of Congress Cataloging-in-Publication Data
Names: Kerpen, Carrie, author ; illustrations by Jessi Chang.
Title: Work it : secrets for success from the boldest
women in business / Carrie Kerpen.
Description: New York : TarcherPerigee, [2018]
Identifiers: LCCN 2017031971 | ISBN 9780143131816 (pbk.)
Subjects: LCSH: Businesswomen. | Women executives. | Career
development. | Success in business. | Women—Vocational guidance.
Classification: LCC HD6054.3 .K423 2017 | DDC 650.1082—dc23 LC
record available at https://lccn.loc.gov/2017031971

Illustrations by Jessi Chang

Printed in the United States of America
1 3 5 7 9 10 8 6 4 2

For Dave, Charlotte, Kate, and Seth,

aka the #bestfamilyever

May our adventures continue, always.

CONTENTS

INTRODUCTION

Leverage Your Assets

I HAVE SOMETHING TO tell you.

Even though this book has "Secrets for Success" in its subtitle, I don't have your secret.

And, unlike most business/self-help/career books, there's not one core philosophy that will claim to change your life in this book.

We all want a magic bullet—the secret that will tell us how to be successful in today's world. We want to know if we should "lean in," call ourselves "badasses," or instead embrace our inner "girl bosses." We search for guidance on how we can build our careers, our families, our looks, our spirits. We buy books, devour articles, follow bloggers, even crack fortune cookies in our search for inspiration wherever we can find it. We are desperate for the tool that will fix whatever is broken within us—that one secret that's guaranteed to help us achieve our goals and dreams.

But there's more than one tool in a toolbox, and there's more than one problem that needs fixing for women today.

The reality is that we are complicated creatures—and we want different things. We don't all want to climb the corporate ladder. We don't all want to be mothers. We each have strengths and weaknesses—different obstacles to overcome. Our stories—and therefore solutions—can be very different.

You may not know me yet, so here's a little background: I'm what you might call an "accidental" entrepreneur. Despite having a rather loud inner self-critic, I built a multimillion-dollar social media agency at a time when there was no one to teach you about social media marketing and I built it without any formal education on how to start or run a business. I never went to business school, and before I started our agency, I didn't have a single day of agency experience. That's just a small taste of my story—one that's built my narrative and philosophies about career and life development. I can (and will) give you the secrets to my own success—but that's only one tool for your kit. You deserve more than one tool.

You, my friend, deserve an entire tool kit.

In this book, I've gathered stories and advice from more than fifty of the boldest and most inspiring women in business. These powerful ladies hail from a wide range of industries, backgrounds, ages, and work experiences. Some are names you know well (Sheryl Sandberg and Barbara Corcoran, for instance); others you may be meeting for the first time. Some have successfully climbed the corporate ladder; others have gone out on their own. Many have done (or are doing) both. All of them, however, will give you tools to WORK IT. But what exactly does that mean?

It's funny: when I told people I was writing a book called *Work It*, they'd jut their hips out to the side, snap their fingers, and strike a "sexy pose." "Work it, girl" they'd say. It is actually hard to say without feeling compelled to move your tush and snap your fingers with sass.

In my world, "working it" has nothing to do with working your "ass," and everything to do with leveraging your "assets." And by assets, I'm not referring to your physical features. I'm talking about the intangible qualities that make you the amazing person you are: your smarts, your experiences, your skills, your strengths and even your weaknesses, your inner light.

The incredible, inspiring women you'll meet in this book all used their unique circumstances, skill sets, and stories to move themselves forward and achieve success on their own terms. They worked with what they had, to create the lives they'd always wanted. Through their stories, they're going to show you how to do this for yourself, too.

Let's start with a story from yours truly—of how I was able to "work it"—to grow my business, my network of women, and my net worth.

This is the story of *All the Social Ladies*.

999,998.
999,999.
Refresh. Refresh. Refresh.
One million downloads.

There I was, sitting in my car, having just pulled into my driveway after taking what felt like the ten-thousandth trip to the orthodontist with my kids. The podcast I had started two years prior had just hit one million downloads. I didn't know how to feel—especially since, originally, I didn't care if a single person listened at all.

You see, this whole thing began two years earlier, when I decided to launch a podcast called *All the Social Ladies*. I didn't start it because I loved Beyoncé—although I definitely do. Really, it was because of two key insights that I've learned about myself over the years.

First, I am a connector. I can find something in common with every single person in a room, and I can also figure out a way to help just about all of them in some capacity. More important, I love doing this. Because of that (and also probably because I tend to come across as friendly and nonintimidating), people have generally labeled me as universally "likeable." It's taken me years to be able to say that, let alone accept that people genuinely seem to like me pretty much instantly, but I've finally learned to stop dismissing it and embrace it as a positive quality. After all, it's part of what made me such a good salesperson throughout my career.

The second important thing I've learned is that I find all of that people energy, socializing and connecting (i.e., the stuff that makes me good at what I do), exhausting. It turns out, I'm an introvert in disguise. I've spent most of my life denying this fact—after all, when you're told over and over that you're gifted at being universally considered "likeable," you need to run with it, and fast. I *was* running, running *away* from facing and dealing with this paradox I felt.

For most of my career and life, I found myself stopping every hour or so to take a bathroom break—only I wasn't going to pee or fix my hair. I was taking breaks to hide from people and for a much-needed breather from the effort I was exerting to connect with them.

And the entire time I was hiding? I was berating myself for needing to.

Yep. No matter how many times I give myself the famous speech from *The Help*—"You is kind, you is smart, you is important"—I still can't fully silence my inner self-critic. My guess is, a lot of you struggle with this, too.

So, what the heck do these things have to do with my creating a podcast named after a Beyoncé song? Let me explain.

My husband, Dave, and I launched our agency, Likeable Media, in 2007. We were in the right place at the right time, really, because we had decided to start a business that created social media content for companies during a year when social media was exploding. Dave was the CEO and I was his number two. Likeable Media quickly became one of the fastest-growing companies in the United States. Six years later, when Dave launched a new company, I became the CEO by default. I'd love to tell you all about how excited I was to be a woman at the helm of this rapidly growing organization in a fast-paced industry, but it wasn't like that at all, at least not at the time.

After an incredible ride from startup to established business under Dave's leadership, times had changed. The market for "social media agencies" was now crowded, and brands were taking their social media management in-house. Also, we had been so busy growing over the past six years, we hadn't figured out how to ensure that the business could actually turn a profit. On top of all that, the heads of other social media agencies were pretty much all the same. Loud. Extroverted. And male.

So there I was, CEO of a company that had been initially heralded as the rising star in social media, hiding and watching it plateau with no clue as to how to move it forward in the changing times. I had two options to choose from. I could either beg Dave to come back—after all, he's loud, he's extroverted, and he's male, so he'd surely know what to do better than I would. Or, I could own this and do something different.

Suddenly, it occurred to me. If I felt annoyed by the constant self-promotion of these chest-beating thought leaders, maybe I wasn't alone. Maybe other women, maybe even potential future clients, might feel the same way.

And here's the lightbulb moment—where I decided to **work it**.

I would start a podcast, and use my people skills to connect with other women in positions of power at their companies. I would ask to interview them and give them a chance to share their philosophies—about social media, and about life as a woman in business. And best of all, I'd get over my "introverted" issue by offering them something that was of value to them. Rather than just bombarding them with a cold email or an awkward greeting at a networking event, I would actually be giving them an opportunity to share their own stories. That settled it—I was launching *All the Social Ladies*.

The original intent behind the podcast was mostly selfish, I admit. My idea was to contact successful women at brands that I wanted Likeable to work with and ask to interview them about social media. I'd slip in a lot of questions that might benefit our company—like, "What are your brand's biggest challenges?" or "Do you use an agency or internal resources for managing your social media?" I also made sure their being on the show added value for them—I'd give them fun social media content featuring quotes from their interviews, which they'd share with their followers.

And slightly selfishly, I figured maybe, just maybe, if they ever needed an agency, they'd think of me.

To my surprise, these powerful women readily agreed to be on my podcast—everyone from Linda Boff, CMO of General Electric, to Sallie Krawcheck, formerly one of the most senior women on Wall Street. I interviewed dozens of women who run digital marketing at Fortune 500 companies, at fashion brands, and at cool startups, and as I did, a couple of interesting things started to happen.

First, my plan worked. I helped these women, and they helped me. The women who were featured were able to use their podcast interviews to get more media coverage—and as their own personal antidote to the "loud male social media story." They had been given a voice—and suddenly, the podcast started growing a loyal fan base of listeners.

Also, business grew. It wasn't instantaneous, of course—none of them concluded their interview with "Oh, I'd love to hire you and Likeable Media." But when they had a need for our services, they remembered our conversation and called me.

As a result of the podcast, from 2014 to 2016 Likeable Media doubled in size and Dave and I tripled our net worth.

Over time, the podcast's topic started to shift. As I interviewed more women, I began to care less about asking them how they use social media in their workplace and more about the stories they were sharing of their careers and their lives. Eventually, I began kicking off the podcast with "Tell me the story of your career"— and I became fascinated with the story of each and every guest. Through the stories of these successful, trailblazing women, I began to find my own confidence and leadership skills in ways I never had imagined. That's when the podcast's listener base started to skyrocket.

As the podcast's audience grew from a few listeners to over a million, it became clear that I wasn't the only one benefiting from these women sharing their experiences and the secrets they'd learned along the way to success. Over the past two years, I have interviewed over two hundred women. I've asked each of them to tell me the stories of their careers—and I've been floored by the stories and the lessons I've learned. Every single woman I've interviewed had something to teach me, and therefore something to teach you.

That's when I realized that maybe their stories needed to be told in a bigger way.

Let's return to 2016—to the scene in the car, where I was sitting in my driveway, hitting refresh, with my three children in the backseat.

As soon as the number changed to one with six zeroes behind it, I blurted out, "One million people have listened to *All the Social Ladies*, you guys! Isn't that amazing?"

"Wait," says Charlotte, my thirteen-year-old. "You have one million *subscribers*?"

"Miranda Sings has six million subscribers," says Kate, my ten-year-old.

"No, no, girls, I have one million downloads. Sorry to disappoint."

"Oh," they say with a shrug.

At that moment, my one-year-old son, Seth, chucks his cookie at my head.

I can always thank my kids for keeping me humble. It was a good reminder that the original intent of this podcast had nothing to do with audience, and everything to do with leveraging my assets and *working it*.

✻

THIS BOOK SERVES as a massive, diverse, personal advisory board of amazing women who want to help you. These powerful ladies have learned how to "work it" in their careers and now they are going to teach you how to do that, too. Now, what exactly does that mean?

Together, we will show you how to leverage your skills, your interests and passions, your strengths and even your weaknesses to create a career and a life you love. You'll learn to work it in your job, in your relationships and friendships, and in your downtime. Equally as important, you'll also learn to identify what will and won't work for *you*—and how to use that knowledge to make your own version of success that fits your goals and dreams.

Of course, I can't tell you exactly *how* you should "work it" in your particular situation; there's no one-size-fits-all answer because the "it" part is different for everyone. But I can (and will) show you how many smart, savvy women have worked it with what they have to create inspiring careers and lives. And I can also give you insights that will help you discover how to get scrappy and work your strengths to succeed against sometimes seemingly insurmountable odds.

We can't control the hand we've each been dealt, so it's our job to decide how we play the game. And we will show you how to play to win.

The book has three sections. Throughout my years of interviewing women, I've identified themes that are woven within all of their narratives. I've divided the book that way, and feature stories from women that fall into three key areas:

Part 1: Work It Professionally gives you all the basics of career planning. The women in this section share all the secrets you need to know to get hired, grow in your career, ask for raises, and more.

Part 2: Work It Passionately explores strategies for getting to the right decisions in life. This section will teach you about achieving success and satisfaction by trusting your gut instinct as much as your rational thinking (and when to rely on one more than the other to make the best choices for yourself).

Part 3: Work It Practically examines all the stuff we're afraid to talk about—and sometimes even to admit to ourselves. In this section, inspiring women share how to navigate specific obstacles and challenges that women specifically face in the workplace. We talk about things like family planning and work/life balance (ha!), how to dress, how we're expected to "behave" in the workplace, how to deal with sexism/discrimination/competition from female coworkers and bosses, and much more.

Each of the three sections of the book is divided into short chapters that explore how to handle various aspects of your career, including opportunities, challenges, and questions you'll likely face at some point. They feature successful women's stories that are designed to inspire you and guide you successfully through any situation you may encounter. You can read these in order or skip around to those that are most relevant to your situation. Want to ask for more money at your job? Head over to "Make That Money, Honey" in the Professional section. Curious to know how other women manage building their families and their careers at the same time? Check out "Figure Out Your Family Plan" in the Practical section. Every person's story ends with her personal advice for how to apply the lessons from her experiences in your own life.

Think of *Work It* ultimately as a resource guide that you can reference when you're going through hard stuff or find yourself in uncharted territory, whether that's in your job, your career, your home life, your family or friendships, or anything else. The reality is that every woman is a treasure chest of countless stories of working it through sometimes insurmountable odds, yet we don't talk to one another about this stuff enough. It's time we commit to talking to each other, helping each other, supporting each other. Because when we do that, we also help ourselves.

Are you ready to WORK IT? Let's go!

PART 1

Work It Professionally

CHAPTER 1

Your Network Is Your Net Worth

IT'S FREQUENTLY SAID that it's not what you know, it's who you know. I've found that to be true more often than not. Many times, when you see someone with a truly "dream job"—part of her journey involved an opportunity that became available because of someone in her network. We all know networking is important, but I'm here to tell you that there's more than one way to do it—and to give and receive the type of networking help we all so desperately need.

My husband, Dave, tells an amazing story about a plane ride he once had that changed his life. He sat down next to someone and talked for hours—that person turned out to be Senator Frank Lautenberg. The senator became a powerful and influential member of Dave's network.

Usually when I travel, I tend to react a bit differently. Whereas Dave had no qualms about approaching Senator Lautenberg and chatting away, I tend to be worried about disturbing someone's private time.

That was certainly my first instinct when I spotted Meredith Vieira in LaGuardia Airport. She was sitting with her husband, Richard, and wearing no makeup. I had long idolized Meredith, particularly for how she navigated her career while caring for her husband with multiple sclerosis. The thought of approaching her in an airport seemed way too intimidating. . . and so I bided my time, staring at her instead for a good, awkward twenty minutes.

When we boarded the same plane, I decided to embrace my inner Dave but in my own Carrie style. I wrote her a note on a napkin and had the attendant pass it up to first class from my lowly coach seat. In it, I talked about my mom and her own struggles with MS. I told her what a champion I thought she was for those of us caring for people with MS and included my email in case she decided she did want to strike up a conversation.

Moments later, I received a response.

Hi, Carrie! Thank you for your very sweet note . . . but my husband is the real champion. He sets the tone in our family and is a constant inspiration . . . when he's not a pain in the ass! I hope your Mom is doing ok. We all know what a bear of a disease MS can be. I wish you the very best. You sound like a wonderful daughter.

Warm Regards,
Meredith

I was in! Without disturbing Meredith too much, I was able to start an email rapport. With high level connections like this, I try to stay in touch often, but not obsessively. I look to nurture the relationship, to always add value, and never to expect something in return.

Remember that when reaching out to someone at a very high

level, you want to establish a sincere personal connection and accept that it may or may not work out. By expecting nothing in return, you avoid disappointment and often end up being pleasantly surprised.

Another celebrity #girlcrush that I had was Sheryl Sandberg—and this was way before *Lean In*. I have followed Sheryl since her days at Google. In 2012, I was heading out to Palo Alto for a client meeting. Palo Alto is home to several tech behemoths, including Facebook—where Sheryl is now the chief operating officer. Every time I heard Sheryl speak—whether in the media or at a conference, I was blown away, and I became fixated on getting a meeting with her while I was in town. I took a chance and sent an unsolicited email to Sheryl with the following subject: "Nothing ventured, nothing gained."

So, I have about thirty seconds to get your attention before you click delete. Here goes nothin'.

–You know my husband, Dave Kerpen, with whom I cofounded Likeable Media. He's very close friends with Randi, and Ed Zuckerberg is on our Advisory Board.

–I have tried to emulate you in my own speeches about women, families, and entrepreneurship. I know you asked for mentor stories on your Facebook page; I've included mine here.

–I am at the Facebook offices on Wednesday 3/28 with my client Medtronic, and I would do absolutely ANYTHING to get to say hello to you.

That's all I've got. Let me know if you're in town, and if nothing else, I hope you know how profoundly you have affected my life and the lives of other women who are in our space. Thank you.

Time passed, and so did my Medtronic meeting. Although I was disappointed, I've trained myself to keep my expectations low around these things—I figured she was just busy and that our paths would cross eventually. One day, this popped up in my inbox:

Carrie—What a lovely email. Thank you—means a lot to me. Do you live in the Bay Area?   —Sheryl

OMG OMG OMG. I was officially freaking out. There's only one issue: I'm never in the Bay Area. I meet with Facebook at their offices in New York, so I have no need to be there. Suddenly, I find myself telling her that I am in the Bay Area *all* the time. We set a date to meet and off I flew.

I waited in the Facebook office lobby for hours as Sheryl got delayed by far more important meetings than one with a young woman who she thought was in the area all the time. The next day, I was scheduled to be class parent at my daughter's school, so even though there was a chance that I'd get to meet Sheryl the next day, I had to respect the boundaries I set for myself as a parent. (Some things trump even the intense desire to meet with one of your idols.)

I flew home, defeated and too embarrassed to let Sheryl know that I flew out just for her.

I knew that even with the smallest "in," it was important to keep up the connection. After all, fostering relationships turns acquaintances into longer-lasting connections. I made sure to continue our rapport for many years after that. She sent me a personalized, autographed copy of *Lean In* and asked what I thought. I sent her updates on Likeable's progress as an agency, and work we did for nonprofits with Facebook that was particularly noteworthy.

When it came time to write my own book, I looked back at the original email I sent her. "Nothing ventured, nothing gained." I decided to reach out to Sheryl, on that old email chain, and tell her about that day in Facebook's lobby—and to reveal my embarrassment. Here a snippet of what I wrote:

> In 2012, I emailed you to meet and you were gracious enough to give me time on your calendar when I said I was in Menlo Park often. The truth was, I had no plans to be in Menlo Park at that time, but the idea of even 15 minutes with you was worth the trip. I flew out, and got there, and was in the office waiting, when you understandably got delayed until later that day. I had a flight booked, and had to get home for my babies. I left without ever getting to chat with you. I still think about that trip often, and despite my disappointment at the time, I would make that trip again in a heartbeat for a chance to talk to you in person.

I asked if she'd be willing to be interviewed for my upcoming book. She wrote back within minutes. Her exclusive interview for this book can be found in the "Make Lemonade" chapter.

This was one of my better examples of activating a powerful person in my network—I expected very little, I made sure to nurture the relationship and follow up, and I looked to add value whenever I could.

Today, everyone, even your biggest business girl crush, is accessible in some way—really, many of them are just one tweet away. If it's possible to get in touch with women at that level, imagine how easy it can be to build a network of women around you already who can help you move forward in your own career.

CARRIE'S TIPS

❋ There are different ways to network. Ditch the perception that it's clunky or awkward and do it in a way that works for you.

❋ Being thoughtful and personal in your communication not only makes you memorable, it also opens doors.

How to Network for Non-Networkers

While I was comfortable networking in a more subtle way, many women fear networking in any capacity at all.

Anya Hoffman, currently the senior editor at Epicurious, recalls when she left her prior job in publishing to pursue her passion for journalism as a freelance writer. As a freelance writer, you have to pitch your pieces to editors, and when Anya was starting out, she had no idea how it worked. She also had an almost paralyzing fear of networking. Unlike full-time employment—when you're freelancing, you really need to land your own writing gigs—without a strong ability to network—you're destined for failure.

Anya's first step in overcoming her fear was to sign up for a large networking group of freelance writers, in the hopes that she could learn from her peers. Members of the networking group recommended that she take the second step—getting formally educated about freelancing. Anya began taking a few courses in freelance journalism—to really learn how the whole thing worked. There she befriended one of the teachers, a freelance writer for *The*

New York Times Magazine and *GQ*. The teacher explained to Anya that it wasn't enough simply to join networks and *hope* contacts would come your way; she needed to actually reach out to members of the network to get anywhere.

Anya made a list of everyone she was remotely connected to in publishing, and she forced herself to email them all and ask to get together for coffee. Some of her contacts were intimidating, and she only really knew them peripherally—like one of the head editors at *New York* magazine. "I absolutely had to *force* myself to do this."

The networking paid off. First, she was able to sell a story to *Marie Claire*. Then, one of her teachers pinged her regarding a story about cricket flour–based protein bars. The teacher didn't have the time to write the piece, so she mentioned it to Anya. Remember that head editor at *New York* magazine who Anya was so reluctant to ask for coffee? Well, Anya wrote the story, sent it, and ended up getting a clip on *New York* magazine's Web site—a highly coveted piece for her portfolio.

Anya continued to build up her clips, and she also expanded her network by joining Facebook groups, including secret groups set up for female journalists and some specifically for food writers. The camaraderie actually felt like she was in an office environment: "It was like having work friends who kept each other accountable."

One day, the editor of *Travel + Leisure* posted in the group. Anya looked her up and saw that she was a fellow Wesleyan alum. Now with a bit more networking experience under her belt, it was a bit easier to reach out. The editor ended up hiring Anya for a regular freelance job at *Travel + Leisure*, where their relationship continued to grow over time. When the editor eventually left *Travel + Leisure*, and Anya's gig was up, she recommended that

Anya contact her husband, who is the executive director of Epicurious. That's how Anya landed at the job she has currently.

"I can say with certainty that if I didn't push myself to network, none of this would have happened," Anya notes, and she's right. It's infinitely easier to get the job you want when you have put in the work to make those kinds of personal connections. It's just up to you to make them happen.

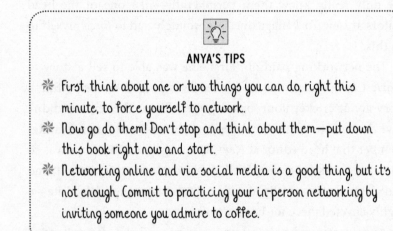

ANYA'S TIPS

❋ First, think about one or two things you can do, right this minute, to force yourself to network.

❋ Now go do them! Don't stop and think about them—put down this book right now and start.

❋ Networking online and via social media is a good thing, but it's not enough. Commit to practicing your in-person networking by inviting someone you admire to coffee.

Make Connecting with Others an Ongoing Priority

As Anya discovered, networking is a skill, and it takes time and practice to get good at it. No one knows this better than Sandy Carter, an industry veteran who has been in the tech world for decades.

Sandy has the perfect blend of big business and startup experience, leading the startup division of a major Fortune 500 tech company. Sandy is also a founding board member of WITI (Women in Technology International). The global networking group helps female entrepreneurs break through the barriers that hinder their success, helping them build connections and identify opportunities for growth.

Sandy believes that everything in life—not just entrepreneur-ship—boils down to who you know and how they can help you get to the next level. It's all about relationships.

How do we form better relationships? Sandy's major tip: Don't view networking as a nice-to-have—view it as part of the job.

The big aha moment came when one of her mentors asked her, "Why do I see you running down to the cafeteria, grabbing lunch, and racing back to your office?" When Sandy responded that she simply had too much work to do to spend time having lunch with her coworkers, her mentor advised: "The next time you're down in the cafeteria, just take a look who's sitting down there."

When she did, she saw that they were mostly men—all having lunch with their colleagues and building important relationships that were helping them move up in their careers. And there Sandy was, "working my booty off back upstairs," ignoring the network-ing part of the job and essentially getting nowhere.

That's when Sandy had an epiphany. "Networking shouldn't be something you do when you have extra time. It's something you have to prioritize."

SANDY'S TIPS

❋ If it's not already naturally one of your job responsibilities, pretend networking is in your job description. It's truly a requirement to succeed in any job.

❋ Don't eat lunch at your desk. Spend that time socializing with others in your organization. You'll get much further that way.

Don't Just Facebook or FaceTime, Get Together Face-to-Face

Even if you're focusing on following Sandy's advice and not eating alone at your desk, so much of networking today takes place online. But while most of our interactions with others seem to be virtual these days, nothing can replace the genuine authenticity of a face-to-face connection. And nobody understands that better than Erica Keswin.

From the time she was very young, Erica loved connecting people. So it was no surprise when she became an executive recruiter at the prestigious search firm Russell Reynolds, and also had a little side hustle where she constantly set up friends on dates. She's a natural matchmaker in every sense.

Because Erica spent most of her career making in-person connections, something big was lit within her when she decided to go see Sherry Turkle speak about her new book *Alone Together: Why We Expect More from Technology and Less from Each Other.* After the lecture, Erica approached Sherry and asked if she needed help on the research she was doing around the impact of technology on connection and culture in the workplace. How was technology affecting watercooler conversations? Networking with peers? Communication with your boss? Erica was ready to find out how to reclaim conversation and connection in the professional world, and Sherry was ready to partner with her and let her try to figure it out. A partnership was born.

Erica got to work—and in her research uncovered a study on firemen conducted by a professor at Cornell University. The study showed that firemen who eat meals together are better at their jobs. It turns out, eating together allowed for more conversation, which led to stronger connections, which led to greater team performance. Suddenly, Erica knew exactly what she had to do to bring back connections in the workplace.

Erica followed her passion, and in 2016 she devoted her time to sharing the science and stories of human connections with global brands, communities, teams, and individuals. Inspired by the research, Erica has made it her business to help people honor relationships. And as a hats-off to the firemen and their go-to firehouse meal, she calls her work the Spaghetti Project.

"When left to our own devices—literally and figuratively—we just aren't connecting," says Erica. We're forgetting how to look each other in the eye and have a real, genuine conversation, which is a critical skill in the workplace, in relationships, and in life in general.

Erica's suggestion for those of us who are still stuck on networking digitally? Dedicate two hours—just two hours in your week—to connecting with people offline. Have coffee, have a chat, go back to the watercooler. You'll be amazed how much more connected your network actually becomes—your relationships will be stronger, as will your communication skills.

ERICA'S TIPS

✳ Put down your phone and talk to the person nearest to you—just for five minutes. Need to start a conversation, but still feeling tied to the digital world? Try asking someone what their favorite emoji is and why.

✳ Eating with colleagues will make your work relationships stronger—and pay off in the long run in terms of your career success and satisfaction. Schedule time with them to go to lunch or dinner.

Make Yourself Memorable

While Erica discovered the importance of connecting face-to-face, Deena Baikowitz was busy making sure that the next generation was armed with the tools to do so.

When Deena walks in the room, you know who she is immediately. Standing just 4 feet 6¾ inches tall, with curly red hair and freckles, she is immediately recognizable. Even though that benefits her today, it was those very aspects of her looks that caused her a great deal of insecurity in high school. As the founder and CEO of the Fireball Network, a training and coaching group dedicated to helping their clients be better networkers, she likes to joke, "Before I was a fireball, I was a frizzball." Rather than let her frizzy, fiery red hair get the best of her, Deena decided to own it and turn it into an asset that would highlight her core strengths, which are connecting people and building brands. She started the Fireball Network, based on her unmissable hair color, and she and her brand quickly became unforgettable. It also taught her the first lesson about networking and brand building: Be *memorable*. That, Deena cautions, is more than being just about your look. "It's about being able to talk about what you do in a way that's different," she says. "I can't tell you how many times I've met people at networking events who say things like, 'Hi, I'm Lisa. I'm a lawyer,' when in fact they are the top business development lawyer at one of the country's largest firms. Or, 'Hi, I'm Joanie, I'm an architect.' That's forgettable. But 'Hi, I'm Joanie, I designed that building down the road over there' is not. So much of networking is dependent on you versus other people. When you think about how to present yourself in an interesting way, you become memorable. When you follow up, you won't be forgotten in a sea of business cards."

I remember when I first watched Deena put this into practice, and saw firsthand the results of how she can take a four-sentence email and turn it into a year's worth of business. Deena had met my husband, Dave, at a networking event, and he recommended that she connect with me. She knew that I was very busy running Likeable, along with a speaking calendar that was full. Deena had set a goal for herself to increase her own speaking engagement bookings, and she was particularly interested in the upcoming Women 2.0 event where I was scheduled to deliver the keynote address. She shot me a four-sentence email.

Sentence 1: Introduction—Who she was, and a fun fact that made her memorable—including how she was referred to me (Dave), and a reference to our height differential (a full sixteen inches)

Sentence 2: What she needed (insight on how to speak at next year's conference)

Sentence 3: How she could offer help in exchange (any networking coaching my young team needed)

Sentence 4: Asking for a specific, easy request (needed fifteen minutes to talk to me on the phone and was willing to wait as long as it took)

This short email was funny, memorable, easy to read, and therefore easy to reply to. I gave her the fifteen minutes, introduced her to the conference organizers and to one of my clients, who hired her to coach their team. In turn, she coached my team on better networking skills. One of my team members who attended the workshop, a writer, used to work at the career Web site Levo

League. She thought Deena might be perfect as a speaker there, too. She spoke there, and a *Forbes* columnist was in the room—who, in turn, has frequently featured Deena as an expert in the networking space. All of this led to exposure and business growth for Deena. And it started by being to the point, in a memorable way.

Deena knows how to work a room, an email chain, a phone, and her specific skill sets to get to her endgame. Her trick to doing all that successfully? "Ask simply, and simply ask."

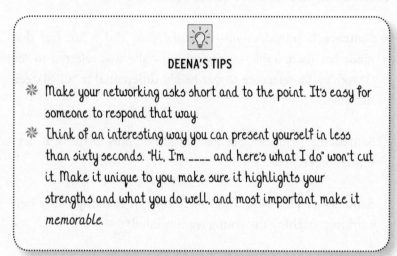

DEENA'S TIPS

❋ Make your networking asks short and to the point. It's easy for someone to respond that way.

❋ Think of an interesting way you can present yourself in less than sixty seconds. "Hi, I'm ____ and here's what I do" won't cut it. Make it unique to you, make sure it highlights your strengths and what you do well, and most important, make it memorable.

EXERCISE ONE

Navigate Your Way to Networking Success

Figuring out how to network is an important piece of the career puzzle. To start your journey, I want you to take the lessons from the ladies in this section and really WORK IT to create the connections you want and need to succeed. Since networking can be a complex path to navigate, I've set up a GPS system to help get you to your networking goals. Try it out and see where it takes you.

Starting Destination: You

Describe yourself in a sentence and why anyone would want to know you. Remember Deena's story—it's not just "Hi my name is _____ and I am a _____." Think about what makes you interesting and sets you apart from others and write down what that is.

....

....

....

....

....

End Destination: Your Desired Contact

List someone you'd like to connect with and why you're hoping to connect with them.

....

....

....

....

....

Now let's activate Your GPS to see if you can get there without too much difficulty:

Gifts to Give
What gifts do you have to offer this person? Forget about how they can help you— how can you help them? Think about these things and rate your value to this person honestly on a scale of 1-10 in the box to the right.

Potential to Connect
Ask yourself the following: How closely connected are you or your contacts to this person? Are you able to find someone who can reach out to this contact on your behalf? If not, do you and your contact have a shared life experience that might make your outreach less cold and more relatable? Rate this potential on a scale of 1–10 in the box to the right.

Simplicity of a Meeting
How easy can you make it for this person to meet with you? (Remember, I flew out to California and sat in the Facebook lobby for hours in the hopes that Sheryl Sandberg would have some free time—that would be a 10.) Rate this potential on a scale of 1–10 in the box to the right.

Scoring

Now see where your rating score falls by adding up these three categories to find out how you can get to this connection or whether it's better to pursue another instead.

24–30: Congrats, this person is accessible to you. Now go WORK IT and create that connection.

12–24: You've got work to do before you WORK IT to this connection. Look at each of the three scores and see how you can build them up. Can you find a commonality that you can share that makes you more relatable, and therefore higher on the "potential to connect" score? Can you take a look at what you have to offer, and maybe find something you hadn't thought of before to increase your "gifts to give" score? Are you attending a conference next year where your dream connection will be speaking? Plant the seeds early so a "simplicity of a meeting" will be more feasible.

3–11: Girl, this desired connection is a bold choice. Keep dreaming and brainstorming as to how you might connect with this person one day, and focus on more attainable contacts in the here and now in order to WORK IT to your goals.

CHAPTER 2

Find Your FAB PAB
(Your Fabulous Personal Advisory Board)

Y OU'VE HEARD FROM a few successful women now about ways to network successfully. But your network alone won't be enough to help you make the right decision in a crucial situation, get through a tough time in your career or life, or figure out how to turn a business idea you have into an actual business. What you also need is a support network, or what I like to call your FAB PAB, your Fabulous Personal Advisory Board.

I originally heard about this concept while at my first management job. I was sent to a fantastic training program, where the facilitator drew a circle on a piece of paper and said to me:

"This circle is a table. Seated at the table are your personal advisory board. List their names."

I was at a loss.

"Do you mean my mentor?" I asked. Weren't leaders of companies and nonprofits the ones who were supposed to have advisory boards? Or maybe entrepreneurs? Since I was neither, I could not figure out why a group of people would sit at a "virtual" table and advise a regular manager like me, let alone on what. Everyone had always told me to seek out a mentor or maybe two—not a whole *bunch* of them—and certainly not about anything other than my career.

Sensing my confusion, the facilitator explained, "Think about the people you go to when you have a challenge—at work, in life, with your partner. Imagine they were all on a board that represented you and your life. They're there to advise you and help you grow, and also to keep you from making mistakes. Who would be on that board?"

What an awesome concept. It dawned on me how much more accessible and achievable this approach is versus the traditional mentor/mentee relationship. The truth is, a formal mentorship is often limited in the support and guidance it can offer. Plus, people often think of seeking out mentors in a career capacity only. You generally choose someone from your industry whom you've met in a work setting. But the reality is, especially as women, we need guidance on a lot more in and out of the workplace than things like how to get a promotion or deal with a difficult boss. We need guidance around managing our families and children, our health and emotional wellness, handling discrimination or sexism, and finding balance, as well as the common career challenges everyone faces. A personal advisory board could offer advice and support on a lot more than one mentor could—helping guide not only my career, but other aspects of my life, too.

I realized I didn't need a formal mentor. I already had an army of people who loved me and would help me. There was Peggy Iafrate, the woman who first told me that I had to get experience in sales. There was Jil Wonoski, who taught me how to negotiate for better pay and was the best manager I had ever known. There was my mother who—despite having no experience in my field of work—always asked the right questions to help me get to the place I needed to be. And there was Dale—one of my college BFFs, who knew me better than I knew myself.

After identifying the first core members of my personal advisory board, my next thought was: How can I help *them*? I wanted to focus on making these relationships mutually beneficial and bringing as much value to their lives as they bring to mine. Over the next few years, I also began seeking out new people who I would consider to be on my personal advisory board. And I started thinking about how I could pay it forward. Which other women could I help to achieve their goals? At which tables would I be seated, and could I make an impact?

❋

SOMETIMES, SOMEONE SERVES on your FAB PAB for quite some time before you can figure out how to truly make the relationship work well for everyone—but then you do, and it's just magic. Such was the case with Candie Harris.

At Likeable, Candie was the client whom I most wanted to be like. She was brilliant, and direct. She was strategic, and she was the kind of leader that you knew people loved working for. She worked at Esselte, a global manufacturer and marketer of office products for over twenty-five years. As you can imagine, the world of paper office products was changing, and Candie, a global vice president at Esselte, was ready for a change, too.

I had been coming to Candie in an informal mentor capacity for many years. I asked her anything and everything—including scenarios involving employees, and what kind of renovation would be best for my kitchen. We became very close friends, and she was an important part of my life.

So when Candie sat down to talk to me about her next move after Esselte, I knew exactly what we should do. I was about to become CEO of Likeable, and I needed a number two. Candie could come to me as my COO and help run the business. She was a former client, so she knew the ins and outs. Also, she could help guide the much younger staff to teach them critical workplace skills that they were lacking in a young startup environment. I wasn't sure that she'd take me up on it—in fact, I was convinced she would retire, since she certainly was in the position to be able to. But it turns out, Candie was thrilled to take on the challenge.

The job was perfect for Candie. She got to do what she loved: guiding young people and helping to give them crucial work and life experience. And she also got to help me make the company more profitable. We joke a lot that our relationship is a lot like Robert De Niro and Anne Hathaway in *The Intern*, especially when she was learning the ins and outs of social media, but the reality is, making our relationship more symbiotic was one of the best things we could have done for each other.

Candie and I never had a formal mentor/mentee relationship. We just helped each other when we needed it most. And if you can find five to seven people in your life who can help guide you—who can sit at your table and you can help each other when you need it most—you've got your FAB PAB.

CARRIE'S TIPS

❋ Stop worrying about finding a formal mentor. Focus on forming relationships with multiple people who can serve as key advisors not only in your work or career, but also in other aspects of your life.

❋ Think about how you can help the people who have helped you.

Create a "Girls Only" Club

I actually credit Candie for encouraging me to branch out and join more networking groups—including the one formed by Rachel Sklar and Glynnis MacNicol, founders of a company called TheLi.st. TheLi.st is an online community of high-powered women in media and tech. It's run as a Google group where you can ask anything and everything and get a response from brilliant women who work in media and tech. They also feature in-person networking events and conferences. Originally, when I joined TheLi.st, I figured it would be a great opportunity to network with other women in my industry. What I found was much more—women who offered advice on everything from childbirth to getting a manuscript published to the best type of undergarments for your figure. With instant access to hundreds of high-profile women, my FAB PAB became even bigger and stronger.

I spoke to Rachel Sklar about what prompted her to form this kind of community in the first place and how the women have served as advisors in her own life. "It started as a way to get ahead of exclusionary, homogeneous networking groups and news coverage for white dudes, and it turned into the go-to brain trust for ambitious, badass women."

TheLi.st also helps its cofounder in lots of ways, some very tactical and specific, like the time Rachel was presented with a brand ambassador opportunity with a clothing brand. She had no real experience with a deal of this size, so she reached out to the members of TheLi.st for advice. The response was astounding. She received replies with detailed instructions on what to do. She received insight from women who had been on the talent end of deals like this as well as those who negotiated similar deals on the brand side. This outpouring of knowledge gave Rachel a much better idea of the market for brand ambassadors as well as a strong sense of her asking power. Based on that one conversation with TheLi.st and the helpful advice its experienced members shared, Rachel successfully negotiated double the initial amount offered to her.

TheLi.st also helped Rachel at one of the most critical—and deeply personal—points of her life, when she became pregnant as a single mother.

When Rachel revealed that she was pregnant and going it on her own, TheLi.st came through in droves—offering advice, support, and supplies. They sent meals, and even formed a night nurse fund. They also helped her to figure out how to structure her "maternity leave," which, in this country, is not a luxury that is afforded to entrepreneurs.

"When I founded TheLi.st, I was keenly aware of what a difference it would have made in my life in my twenties and early thirties to have had an organization like this, but it never would have occurred to me that all the reasons I thought TheLi.st would help me would pale in comparison to how it helped me figure out how to manage being a single mother and having a career."

Rachel is now the proud mother of Miss Ruby Sklar, age two, the youngest member of TheLi.st. Ruby is fortunate—she has an army of women around her. But the reality is, you can, too. You just have to seek them out.

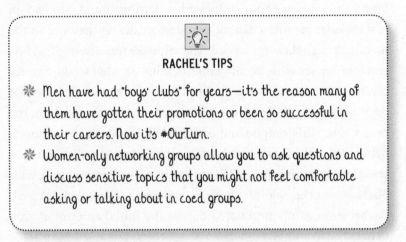

RACHEL'S TIPS

❊ Men have had "boys' clubs" for years—it's the reason many of them have gotten their promotions or been so successful in their careers. Now it's #OurTurn.

❊ Women-only networking groups allow you to ask questions and discuss sensitive topics that you might not feel comfortable asking or talking about in coed groups.

Follow Through and Follow Up

Finding groups like TheLi.st is one way to broaden your FAB PAB, but it's only one way of many. In fact, one of the biggest questions I get from young people is exactly how to find people to serve on your FAB PAB, specifically early in your career. It is significantly easier than you think. Just ask Morgan Greco, vice president, social media business development at HISTORY, Lifetime, A&E, and FYI.

At the beginning of her career, Morgan was (and still is) an introvert. She had studied at Penn State, and, thanks to an internship, she knew that she wanted her first job to be at Viacom. She did what anyone these days can do: she logged in to LinkedIn to find people who worked there and connect with them. Morgan did a search for people who worked at Viacom and also graduated from her alma mater. She sent out emails to fifty alums, offering to buy each of them a cup of coffee in exchange for an informational interview or a chat about their experiences working at the communications giant.

Only one person responded: a top-level senior executive who worked in finance. Even though she wasn't interested in finance, Morgan decided to schedule the meeting anyway. But she was a nervous wreck that it would be a huge waste of his time. So she decided to ditch the idea of simply asking him if he could "get her a job at Viacom," as she knew most people do in these kinds of informational interviews. Instead, she asked a bigger question— one that had been weighing on her mind for a while.

"I asked him, 'You're obviously at the top of your career, and very successful. How important is an MBA? Should I delay work and pursue my higher education?'"

His advice was loud and clear. "Skip it," he said. "Go for industry experience, and continue to network just like you did today." He was so impressed with her ability to reach out and get this meeting that he placed a call to HR, looking for available positions that might be a fit for Morgan.

With one phone call, this executive was able to get Morgan's foot in the door at Viacom. She aced the interview and her dream career became a reality.

As Morgan grew in her career, she wanted to give back in the same way the executive had helped her to get to where she wanted to be. Now a VP for three major media brands, Morgan speaks across the country at conferences for women in advertising, television, and social media. At every one, she's swarmed by young women who ask for her card or ask if they can follow up with her. Every time, she hands out her card and says "Call me."

Of the approximately fifty women she offers to help at each conference, how many do you think call and set up follow-up time? Usually one. Occasionally two.

"I used to be afraid that I would get inundated by offering to help these women. But now I see that the path is clear for young people who truly take advantage of the opportunities in front of them. Do what most people don't—follow up!"

MORGAN'S TIPS

✳ If you want to switch jobs or careers, start with a search on LinkedIn—or even better, your alma mater's alumni network (or even your high school's alumni network if there is one). Search for alumni who work at your dream company or in your dream industry and reach out and ask them for an informational interview.

✳ When someone hands you a business card and offers you help in your career, follow up.

EXERCISE TWO

Finding Your FAB PAB

You may instinctively know who sits at your "table" and serves as your board of advisors—but let's put it to the test and find out who deserves one of those coveted seats. First, write down who you think would be on your FAB PAB. Then read through the scenarios below and decide who you would really call on to work through each of these challenges and write their name(s) in the corresponding boxes to the right of each situation in which you'd call them. These are the people who should truly be on your FAB PAB. Compare them to your original list and note any discrepancies. Who is missing from your table who deserves a seat and vice versa?

Who Do You Call . . .

When you have a big idea—and you need someone to tell you it's great, but also to help you make it better.

....

....

When your boss tells you that your chances of getting promoted are slim to none.

....

....

When your bae tells you they just want to be friends.

....

....

When you want to buy that Prada bag, but aren't sure if you should cash in your 401(k) to do so.

....

....

When you have an industry-specific question about the project you're working on.

....

....

When you need someone to bail you out of jail, and help you over the border! (Kidding, sort of.)	....
When you absolutely, positively must meet Oprah, and you need a path to get to her *now* ...	....
... and when a few minutes later you need a reality check: No, meeting Oprah is not happening today.	....
When you're thinking about leaving your investment banking job to open a bakery.	....
When you need to hear that you're the best, because you're feeling at your absolute worst.	....

A few things to note: Your FAB PAB will be far more helpful and beneficial to you if it consists of at least three people minimum whom you can turn to for support in various situations. If you have listed only one person for all of these scenarios, it's possible that you have walls up about seeking help from others. (Either that, or you just REALLY like that one person, I guess!) Consider picking a few people that you'd like to be on your board, and find something you'd like to ask them about—a fifteen-minute coffee date can do wonders.

I also want to make sure you're giving back—so let's look at how you might be able to help when you're sitting at someone else's table. What advice are you asked to give most often? Write it down in the blank space provided at the end of the sentence below.

People usually come to me for help with

....

Keep this in mind for when you're asked to support others in this way or similar ways and volunteer. Your support will be repaid in kind.

CHAPTER 3

Get the Gig

STARTED MY CAREER in marketing—and then took a chance on a sales position at Radio Disney. Radio Disney turned out to be one of the best career and life decisions that I ever made—not only did I learn that I had sales skills, but I also met my husband there! Eventually, I thought I would leave Disney to try my hand at sales management. In retrospect, this was not the best move for me—especially since I valued control over my time above all else (when you work in sales, you have a lot of flexibility if you're making your numbers), and I always hated administrative stuff. But ambition is a powerful driver, and I wanted to grow in my career beyond just monetarily. I wanted to take on more, and gain new skills.

I went into the lobby of Cox Media, where I was applying for the sales manager position—and I did what I always do. I made BFFs with the receptionist. Soon we were talking about curly hair products, what she brought for lunch that day, and how she wanted to redecorate the front area. I saw an older man watching me from afar, with a sort of wistful, amused smile. I smiled back, and went in for the interview with the HR manager.

At Cox Media, once you were approved by the hiring manager, you had to pass a phone screener test. I was asked a seemingly endless series of random questions via phone by an outside sales consulting group. These questions were really bizarre:

> *"A baby is crying on an airplane that you're sitting on for the next four hours. What do you do?"*

> *"Do people have a right to their own opinions? If so, do you have a right to change them?"*

I remember that last question in particular, because I thought I gave an amazing answer. Something about Oprah, and believing that people need to be their best selves . . . I was channeling my inner Buddha for these responses. I was going to be the best manager ever!

When I told my husband about the call, I saw his lip twitch a bit. "Carrie, people have a right to their opinions, but no matter what, it's your *duty* to change them if you feel differently. That's the answer they want." It shows you're a salesperson with high command—you own every room you walk into.

This made no sense to me. I'd built my sales career off of listening—and if someone felt differently than I did, I would work with them to come to a place of common understanding. I'm basically freaking Oprah here, why was my answer wrong? But I knew that Dave was more of a traditional salesperson than I was, so he was probably right.

The next day, I got a call from Julie Sells, the woman whom I would be reporting to if I got the job. She told me that I failed the screener. While I had high scores in many areas, ironically it was the area of "sales command" that didn't meet the threshold for hiring.

I wanted to hide my head in the sand. It took me seven years and over a million dollars in commission to feel like a good salesperson—and now a test from a sales consulting company confirmed my worst fear—I sucked.

After a brief pause, Julie spoke again:

"You know, even though you didn't pass the screener, I am able to break the rules this one time and hire you for the position. My boss's boss was in town on the day of your interview—and he saw you talking up the receptionist. He feels that is the true test of a great salesperson, and a great manager. Let's do this."

I took the job, managed my first team ever, and we beat our numbers by 30 percent that year.

CARRIE'S TIPS

❋ Don't base your self-worth on one data point like a score on a test that may not effectively evaluate or test for your true abilities and skills.

❋ Act like every single person in the building could be your hiring manager.

Be a Super Sleuth

To get your foot in the door, you can use my method of making friends with the receptionist, or you can help yourself to a healthy dose of super sleuthing. Take it from Lyndsay Signor, currently the senior director of consumer engagement at NBC Sports Group.

Today, Lyndsay oversees the social strategy for all properties within NBC Sports and NBC Olympics. Basically, she's currently holding what's considered to be a dream job. So, how did she get there? By keeping her eye on the prize, and watching the job openings at NBC like a hawk.

As Lyndsay's college graduation neared, she didn't have a clear idea of what she wanted to do afterward, but she knew where she wanted to be—and that was New York City. So with no job lined up and with the money she saved from waiting tables while in school, she followed her gut and moved to New York with the hopes of finding a career that she'd fall in love with—a gamble that eventually paid off. Lyndsay got her foot in the door at NBC as a page, a twelve-month hands-on development program that allows you to work in all different parts of NBC.

Her first assignment was with the NBC Sports Corporate Communications Group, working on PR. As a page, you spend very little time at each post, but Lyndsay, a sports enthusiast, was determined to get a job in this department. So, she kept in touch with the team, with her eyes set on a coordinator position for the Olympics. The job was a twelve-month rotation—meaning each person only stayed in the role for a year. The position was currently filled, but she knew when the person in the spot had accepted the position, and she knew their year was almost up. She followed the job posting closely, knowing that they would soon have to replace it. When it was time, she pounced, and ended up working for NBC Sports at the Beijing Olympics.

Once Lyndsay discovered the secret that being a bit of a super sleuth and doing your detective work can lead to being in the right place at the right time, she also discovered that you can create the right time if you can simply find the right reason.

When Lyndsay returned to the States, her boss had taken on all PR, marketing, and promotions. Lyndsay was the lowest person on the totem pole, but she knew that she could find a way to add value and create a sense of urgency. She mentioned the importance of Facebook and Twitter to interact with *Sunday Night Football* fans. Her boss wound up backing the idea, the program producer jumped on board—and that was the start of the NBC Sports social media team—with Lyndsay at the helm of their small initial test-and-learn strategy. Eventually, Lyndsay became the head of social media for NBC Sports.

While it's true that some of this came down to timing, Lyndsay credits a big part of her success to finding the opportunity and making a case for it. And that's really at the essence of "sleuthing" to get the gig you want. Lyndsay's opportunities didn't simply fall in her lap, she *made* them happen.

So if there's a position or a company you're interested in and know is right for you but it's not available quite yet, consider trying a bit of light, polite stalking. Get in contact with people who work in the position you eventually want to be in or at the company you would love to work for. Ask them how they got there, what skills or knowledge you can develop that will help you get there, too, and/or if there's anything you can do for them. Informational interviews can be incredibly helpful in this regard. "People love talking about themselves," Lyndsay reminds us. Don't hesitate to send a cold email and find out what someone does, how they got to where they are, and what career advice they can offer. Most people, if they have the time, will be happy to oblige. And once you make that connection, you have the go-ahead to follow up to keep in touch (and keep tabs on any openings). You have to be persistent to get your foot in the door.

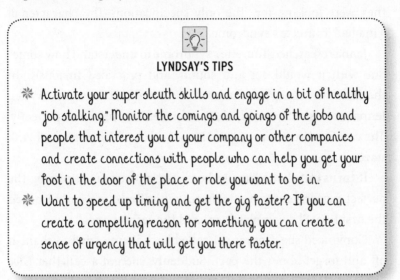

LYNDSAY'S TIPS

❋ Activate your super sleuth skills and engage in a bit of healthy "job stalking." Monitor the comings and goings of the jobs and people that interest you at your company or other companies and create connections with people who can help you get your foot in the door of the place or role you want to be in.

❋ Want to speed up timing and get the gig faster? If you can create a compelling reason for something, you can create a sense of urgency that will get you there faster.

Shake off the No and Keep Pushing Forward

Sometimes no matter how much preparation you do to get a job, you still may hit an obstacle that causes you to screw up so badly. But instead of shrugging and saying "What's the point?," try to shake it off, pull yourself together, and keep pushing forward. Few women demonstrate resilience in their careers like actress Jenna Ushkowitz—most famous for playing Tina on the hit TV series *Glee*.

The role of Tina on this hit show was arguably the one that defined Jenna's career. She was performing in *Spring Awakening* on Broadway when they began holding auditions in New York for a "new musical TV show." At the time, she knew very little about it—and had no idea what a breakout hit it would become.

Jenna, who is of Korean descent, was called in for the role of Tina. "At the time, Tina had no specific ethnicity. I was in there with all of my friends—blondes, brunettes—I had no idea what they were looking for. The only specification? The character of Tina had Tourette's syndrome."

Jenna researched Tourette's syndrome to understand how someone with it would act and sound, and practiced furiously. In the audition scene, the character Tina had just two lines. When Jenna was asked to read, she performed her first line perfectly. The casting director prompted her, "And . . . ." Jenna gave a blank stare.

It turns out that Jenna, in her intense focus on delivering the perfect performance of a teenager with Tourette's, only learned the first line. She completely missed the second one.

Convinced she'd never get called back, Jenna tried to shake it off and forget about the part. Suddenly, she got a call that *Glee* cocreator Ryan Murphy wanted her to come back and sing for a second audition for the role of Tina. Thrilled, she got her song ready and marked up the music in pencil, to guide her on the new cut of the song. There was only one problem—when she got in front of Ryan, it smudged.

Jenna's singing was off tempo—so she did what actresses are told to do when something like this happens: glare at the accompanist, and make it seem like it's his fault. As it was clearly her error, that didn't work. When the audition ended, Jenna left convinced that *Glee* was not to be her gig.

But Jenna ended up securing the role of Tina. Want to know how she did it?

During the audition process, Ryan Murphy had asked her to improv a little bit, since Tina had only two lines in the pilot and he wanted to see more of what the actors trying out for her could do. At the audition, Jenna made up a story about Tina and her mom—how her mom thought glee club would be therapeutic for her stutter, and an opportunity for her to make friends. Ryan loved the positivity of her message, and that's what got her the role on the show that was to become an Emmy-winning phenomenon.

Looking back, Jenna sees one key parallel between theater and other industries—resilience. "When you're not feeling confident or like things will go your way—just push forward."

Another great example of this for Jenna was when she was called to audition for *Waitress*—the hit Broadway show based on the film of the same name. She was living in Los Angeles at the time, and they asked her to send a tape of her singing a song from the show. She wasn't happy with sending a tape, because it's not indicative of what your performance will be like, but she did it anyway. Once she sent it, they came back asking her to rerecord it multiple times. She went through about four iterations, until they finally told her, "We don't think you're right for the role." Jenna was devastated.

About a year later, they called Jenna and asked her to come for a live audition the next day with the creative team. She was apprehensive after a tough few months of auditions, but pushed forward. She was hired that day to replace the current actress who played her role.

Jenna credits her tenacity, the ability to shake off the no and keep pushing forward, as the key to her success in this ubercompetitive field. "So much of it is talent, timing, and a little luck. But the ability to keep going is essential."

JENNA'S TIPS

❋ The ability to "shake off the no" is key to succeeding in a field with a lot of rejection. (And what field doesn't have that?) So keep persevering and pursuing your dream. It will pay off eventually.

❋ There are three "T" factors in your success: talent, timing, and tenacity.

Get Creative in Your Job Application and Nail the Interview!

If I'm looking for someone to help you get the gig of your dreams, I'm going to turn to an expert—one who's hired hundreds of people throughout her career. Meet Brianna Foulds, currently the director of talent acquisition at Cornerstone OnDemand, a leader in cloud-based human capital management software.

As a recruiter, Brianna has seen many applicants come and go, and she knows what gets people hired. Fortunately, she's sitting at your table today . . . so she's able to share lessons from the stories she's seen as a recruiter. Here are Brianna's best tips for helping you cut through the clutter and stand out from everyone else.

1. First, get creative. Brianna has received incredibly creative applications over the years. She remembers: "One guy sent in a 'Mountain Dude' bottle with his résumé wrapped around it." At a "surf 'n' turf" interview event, another candidate plastered his résumé to a surfboard so that he could be in the water with a recruiter and easily reference his qualifications.

Don't be afraid to go the creative route. It clearly makes you memorable. (Years later, Brianna vividly remembers these candidates and can actually recall their names.) While you definitely need the experience and the knowledge base to back it up, being creative with your application will give you a leg up on the competition.

2. Then, nail the interview. Having interviewed countless candidates over the course of her career, Brianna has insight into what makes a great interview. Here are her tips:

   - **Do your research.** It's important to know about the company and the role you're applying for. Make sure you come armed with questions about what the job will entail. Understand the job description and its gaps—focusing on what you might need to learn to be ready for the role. Reach out to people in similar roles, and ask to pick their brain.

   - **Show confidence.** Think of interviewing like going on a date. If you come across as confident in yourself, you'll appear more attractive to the company—and make them feel confident in you, too. Get to the point where they're saying, "Wow, this person really knows what they're talking about."

   - **Ask yourself if it's a good fit.** Remember, it's not just about whether or not the company wants you, it's also about whether or not you want the company. Work should evoke passion for what you love, and at the end of the day, you only want to take a job that works for you.

3. Foster relationships. Organizations tend to be reactive versus proactive when building relationships with potential candidates. They're typically only recruiting for the jobs that are currently open and not thinking about the ones that are

going to open. But forward-thinking companies go beyond the here and now. Personally, Brianna has connected with someone and reconnected four years later once the perfect job came around. Guess what? It's the same for you as an applicant.

It's much easier to get a job when you don't need one—and much harder to get a job when you are desperate. Her advice to applicants: Find your dream company. Stay in touch and nurture the relationship over time. You never know when your dream job will be presented to you.

BRIANNA'S TIPS

❋ Remember, it's not just about if the company wants you. It's about if you want the company, too. #justlikedating

❋ Even if you don't get the job you want, stay in touch. You'll be memorable when the time is right.

CHAPTER 4

Make That Money, Honey

IT DRIVES ME crazy that my friends and I are more comfortable talking about our sex lives than how much money we make. It astounded me that I could recite each of my coworkers' favorite television shows—but I had no idea if any of them contributed to their 401(k). And growing up—we never dreamed of asking our parents how much they made. The reason? We are trained from a very early age that money is a taboo topic—and that's holding us back big-time.

When we share our experiences with money, we come to better understand money. When we come to better understand money, we can make educated choices about money. When we can make educated choices about money, we become much more powerful.

I've had interesting exchanges around money over the course of my career. The first one that I can remember took place right when I was graduating from college and got my very first job offer. I was interning at Radio Disney in Boston—which I loved. I could hardly contain myself when I sat down to discuss an offer of employment. I sat across from a man from Radio Disney's headquarters, which at the time were in Dallas, Texas.

"Darlin'," he said. "You do a real good job here at Radio Disney. I'd love to have you here. I can offer you nineteen thousand dollars a year. I think you'll be real happy here, and I look forward to having you on board."

I made two decisions that day. First, I turned down the job—it simply wasn't enough money to live on. Second, I made it a point to stay in touch with everyone from Radio Disney throughout my career. It turns out, years later, I did return to Radio Disney, but in a sales capacity—and I became the number one salesperson in the country. I made a lot more than $19,000 a year.

Another money story took place midway through my career. I was going to interview for a dream job at Polaroid—working on their I-Zone camera for teenagers. This was right in my wheelhouse, and I was excited at the potential to earn more money. The job I was leaving paid about $40,000 a year. I really connected with my potential boss at the interview. After an amazing interview, she wrote a note on a Post-it, passed it to me, and said, "Okay, we're going to meet my boss now."

When I opened the folded Post-it note, it said, "Tell her you're making 55K now, and you won't come to Polaroid for less than 60K."

I followed her advice, and I got the job. If my future boss Jil hadn't passed me that note, I never would have negotiated for more money—I would have taken whatever they offered with a smile. Learning to value myself and my expertise took time—and it took women like Jil to help me get there.

My third money story was the scariest, but also the most important. Dave and I became entrepreneurs in 2007, and neither of us had ever taken a business class, let alone run a company before.

One night, about two years into running our company, I found myself sitting up in my bed. I thought I was having a heart attack. Turns out, it wasn't a heart attack at all. It was, however, my first full-fledged panic attack. I had just taken the last $10,000 out of our personal savings account—and transferred it to our business checking, in order to meet payroll for the thirty-something people whose livelihoods Dave and I were now responsible for. We didn't have enough in business checking, and it turns out, the exact amount we needed to make up the difference was the exact amount we had in our emergency savings fund.

There was only one problem. Payroll was coming again in two weeks.

It all seemed impossible. The company was doing well. We were adding clients. Things on paper seemed great—but theory and cold hard cash are two different things. Let me explain: In order to keep up with growth, you have to invest. You need to have money to make money, and in my business, when we would win a client, we'd have to staff it and kick it off way before we ever saw a dollar from that client. And here's the real tragedy: The bigger the client, the more they'd need, and the longer they'd take to pay.

I had limited experience in finance, sure, but I knew that there had to be a better way than this. I decided that it was time for a change. I started by getting educated—by talking to advisors and other entrepreneurs and coming clean about my company's financial struggles. Based on their advice, I made a list of next steps. I applied for and secured a good credit line. I started to slow my payments to vendors, matching the speed of my clients' pay cycles. I rewrote my contracts to have slightly better payment terms. And I set a staff-to-revenue ratio that did force me to let a few people go. I also took the world's simplest online finance class— which showed me that I did, in fact, know how to run a business, and that these struggles were something almost all entrepreneurs experience. While it was hard, I was infinitely happier being more disciplined, and have stopped having panic attacks in the middle of the night. I'm also proud to say that we never took outside funding to run the business—and I think that's largely because of the discipline I learned while having to reroute the money train.

CARRIE'S TIPS

* Know your number—know what you want to make, and what number you need in order to say yes to an opportunity.
* Have a money conversation with your friends—practice talking with ease about where you are today and where you want to go.
* Discipline around money is key in business and in life.
* If you're starting a business, get educated on the topic of cash flow and how to manage it. It's different than running your home finances.

How to Fund Your Business Idea

Likeable never needed outside money to support our business. But what happens when you have an idea that you're passionate about, and you don't have enough personal funds to make that dream a reality? Meet Julia Pimsleur, entrepreneur and fundraising superstar.

Julia grew up bilingual in French and English, and felt it gave her an advantage in life. However, when she had her own children, she was surprised to come up empty-handed when searching for a kid-friendly language learning program. Since no one else was providing what she needed, she decided to create it herself. Her ed-tech company Little Pim was born—a multimedia series and set of products featuring an animated panda who teaches young children a second language.

Julia took in about $400,000 in angel investment from friends and family to create her first set of videos, and, a few years later, once her kids were out of preschool, set out to raise the much-harder-to-get venture capital dollars. That turned out to be much harder than raising angel money—and was very discouraging. Julia would pitch at meeting after meeting, and get rejected each time. Eventually, cash was running low.

Julia finally had a meeting set up with a venture capitalist who she was positive would invest. She had connected with the investor previously, and he had a child who was bilingual. He totally got the importance of early language learning—and Julia was sure this would be the one to say yes. She vigorously prepared for the meeting—putting together PowerPoint decks, memorizing every possible critical number, and perfecting her pitch.

Within minutes of walking into the room, she knew she wasn't getting an investment from this group.

Julia's contact brought his boss, and the boss didn't get or appreciate foreign language learning for kids. He kept calling the DVD series "CDs" and looked like he was ready to get up and walk out before she was past her third slide. The meeting was a total bust.

With both her cash and her spirits low, Julia slunk back to her office to tell her team that she had failed. As she walked in, she saw her two key employees huddled together, enthusiastically planning the holiday marketing campaign. In that moment she decided it wasn't going to be a question of *if* she would raise the money—it was a question of *when* she would raise it. She was not going to let her dreams die, or let her team lose out on making a phenomenal product that could help children learn. She determined that she would push past the many rejections and keep raising until she found the right funders.

Julia was relentless in her pursuit of funds, and went on to raise $2.1 million in venture funding for Little Pim; the funds catapulted the company forward into the elite group of women-owned businesses that make it past the million-dollar revenue mark. This proved to be an eye-opening experience in more ways than one for Julia.

Julia found out while fundraising that only 4 percent of venture funding gets invested in women-owned businesses. And most women start their businesses with about 60 percent of the capital that most men do. The results are that male-run businesses on average grow much larger, and much faster, than women-owned businesses do. In fact, she learned that women-run businesses make about 27 percent of what male-owned businesses make in their exact same industry.

When looking at why, Julia realized that many women are intimidated by fundraising, in part because they don't have the same networks that men do. Their access to angel investors and venture capitalists are limited, and as a result, they feel it's just not possible.

With that in mind, Julia started teaching in-person and online workshops on the side to help women do what she had done—raise capital to go big. Some of my favorite nuggets of advice from Julia for women who want to fundraise are:

- Know ahead of time exactly what you'd do with the money if you get it—and be prepared to show potential investors how that investment will help the company grow.

- Realize that more than 50% of your time will be spent fundraising—it's the CEO's job. Make sure you have a team to back you up.
- When you're going to meet with investors, make sure you look as much like them as possible. As superficial as it may sound, it works. Wear what they wear and talk how they talk.

Over the course of three years, Julia helped seventy-five women raise a collective $15 million in capital for their businesses and was inspired to write her book *Million Dollar Women: The Essential Guide for Female Entrepreneurs Who Want to Go Big*. This was the start of her new mission: to help one million female entrepreneurs achieve $1 million in revenue by the year 2020.

JULIA'S TIPS

☀ Fundraising can help you grow a much bigger business, and the opportunity is ripe for women to raise.

☀ Hearing "no" can feel overwhelming, but you must get used to it if you ever want to get to a "yes."

How to Hustle to Make Ends Meet

Sometimes, fundraising is not an option. In that case, you need to hustle. Nikki Ostrower is my friend and my nutritionist, and she's also a woman who gets it **done**. As the founder of NAO Nutrition, she helped me with my own health challenges. Nikki's husband, Matt, had been laid off from his high-profile job in the music industry right before they started trying to get pregnant. They decided to proceed, feeling that the time was right for their family, and that "the universe would provide."

Nikki became pregnant right away, and was hit with perpetual morning sickness. Suddenly, she had to hire another nutritionist to serve her clients while she focused on her health. Matt was receiving job offers, but they weren't the perfect fit. Nikki and Matt decided to wait it out and rely on their savings during the pregnancy.

Emma was born in a beautiful home birth, exactly like Nikki wanted. She immediately started feeling better. Still, Matt was struggling. The job offers he was getting just weren't right, and Nikki really wanted him to find something that was more "right than just right now." They lived in the West Village, not exactly an inexpensive part of New York City, so Nikki had to figure out how to support her family on a single income—if only for a little while.

Perhaps it was out of necessity, or just a plain stroke of genius, but Nikki decided to not only focus on her own time as a personal nutrition coach, but to invest in two areas: ALCAT testing and corporate wellness. The ALCAT test is a food sensitivity test, the results of which can help determine which foods and other substances trigger inflammation and other symptoms. With the current rise of gluten and dairy sensitivities, this test was a definite benefit for those trying to live healthier lives.

Nikki knew that a nurse could administer the test and have someone in and out of the office in fifteen minutes. Because very few businesses are certified to do this, she knew she had a unique benefit as well. She started advertising the service, and voilà, the money started pouring in.

Next up, Nikki targeted the financial institutions of New York. She figured that she could do corporate wellness sessions. Not only that, but financial institutions and investment banks were so focused on wellness, they might consider offering the ALCAT test to their employees. The next thing she knew, Nikki was booking corporate sessions with companywide ALCAT testing. She went from booking single sessions of nutrition work at $200 a session to $45,000 corporate programs. The best part? Nikki was not only making money; she was continuing to do mission-based work, keeping her clients happy and healthy.

Nikki's intense focus on high-value, high-margin products was responsible for getting her through the most intense year of her life. After all, let's not forget it was also her first year as a mother. Looking back now, it's hard for her to believe she got through. But she did—and not only did her husband land a great job, but she launched her very first wellness center in 2017.

NIKKI'S TIPS

※ Necessity is the mother of invention. Think about what you could do today to bring in more money if you had to.

※ Find a unique value that you can provide and you'll be able to command a premium price for it.

Get a Money Mentor

So much of making the right choices around money comes from getting good advice about money from someone you trust. Michelle McKinnon is a financial advisor with Payne Capital Management, which makes sense since she's "always been a little bit obsessed with money." I asked her where that came from, and she didn't skip a beat.

"My mom."

Michelle's mom was not only an amazing role model—raising her family while building her career as an accountant—but she also taught Michelle a critical lesson that many women miss early on: Money is not to be feared.

For Michelle, that meant sitting at the kitchen table with a mock checkbook provided by her mom and a fake bank account that she needed to balance. "I remember when I was six I'd sit with her for hours, balancing checkbooks—hers was the real one and mine, well, not quite as real."

Michelle learned early on that having a money mentor—someone you can talk openly with about money—is key. For Michelle, it was easy—her mother was a professional accountant. For others, it's not always so. "As women, we're afraid to talk about money—about the need to make it, and how we can make more of it. We're taught it's not polite. When you work with someone you trust, they can help you navigate the areas that are harder to do on your own."

As a financial advisor, Michelle had to teach herself that lesson as well. In 2011, she was at a point where she was feeling really down about the market. She'd seen several economic crashes and watched people lose their money. "I was really, really low, and contemplating getting the heck out of this business. That was the *exact* moment for me to lean in and invest." It turns out, Michelle's philosophy, which is shared by her colleagues at Payne Capital, is to "buy low, sell high." It turns out, there's more to that philosophy than just financial. "I was feeling really low, and like there was no hope. That's the exact moment the market turns. Right when you think it never will. So when your gut is down, it's time to buy."

Of course, that's easier said than done, and Michelle had to literally put her money where her mouth was. So, in 2016 when the market collapsed again, Michelle placed 100 percent of her contributions into the single lowest-performing fund at the time. "I wanted to throw up several times," Michelle said. "But I needed to put the 'buy low, sell high' philosophy into place." It turns out that this move, albeit a very risky one that she generally doesn't recommend to clients, paid off tenfold. When the fund started performing, she sold it. "Now, when I share my philosophy, I'm speaking from direct experience versus a more cerebral, intellectual approach. It makes people feel like I've been in their shoes— because I have."

Michelle was so excited to use her "buy low, sell high" strategy, she ran right back to her money mentor to tell her. "My mom was not an investor, she was an accountant, so I felt like I was delivering her this ingenious philosophy that only I knew. She took one look at me and said, 'Michelle . . . duh. This isn't just a money philosophy, it's a life philosophy. When you're down? Keep going and push even harder. When you're up? Consider quitting while you're ahead.'"

Turns out, sometimes the best money advice can be great life advice as well.

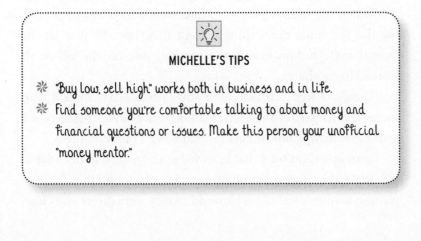

MICHELLE'S TIPS

❋ "Buy low, sell high" works both in business and in life.

❋ Find someone you're comfortable talking to about money and financial questions or issues. Make this person your unofficial "money mentor."

Ask for the Raise

Okay, you've heard a lot from me on investing, on hustling as an entrepreneur, and on fundraising. But what about plain old negotiating when it comes to money and your career? Cara Friedman, now the director of community at ClassPass, was one of Likeable Media's first employees. Over the years, I've watched Cara become the consummate career woman, and I wanted to check in and see what she'd learned over the years. It turns out, she'd learned a whole lot.

Cara told me the number one thing that she's learned to do when talking about money with people in positions of power. "Own the awkward."

Cara takes her awkward feelings around conversations about money and uses them to her advantage. Take the topic of salary negotiations. "I remember that someone once told me that when you're on a phone interview, ask the salary of the job, and put yourself on mute." Cara tried it on the first interview she had after hearing that advice, and it worked. She might ordinarily have interrupted, making excuses for why she wanted more, or commenting. Instead, she let the hiring manager do all the talking. And when she went for her next interview, which was in person, she did the same exact thing, except this time she just hit the mental mute button versus the physical one on the phone. It worked like a charm.

"There's power in making the other person have to deal with the awkward part of the conversation," Cara says. "That's how I learned: watching how others reacted when I put it on them."

Turns out, Cara took that knowledge and used it to her advantage in negotiating raises and promotions. She found that the people who communicated best around money were direct and clear, and metrics oriented. So Cara decided to practice that type of communication with her boss, every single week. "I started by asking what specifically it takes to grow into a new role and earn more money here. I hit my mental mute button and let her talk. Every week, I would follow up with a simple 'How am I doing? Am I working toward these goals?' question." Cara says that while at first this might feel awkward, eventually you get used to it and your boss does, too. And, best of all, it eliminates any surprises.

Finally, Cara feels it's very important to know your worth. For Cara, that means lots of research. She doesn't, however, look at salary bands of positions at her own level. She looks at positions one level up. "That's what I aspire to be, so why not?" says Cara. "I want to know what I'm working toward, and I want to stretch myself to get there."

Judging from Cara's career path, it looks like her strategy is working. Promoted multiple times, she currently heads up social media for all of ClassPass, a fitness startup that has disrupted the fitness industry.

CARA'S TIPS

✳ Practice having uncomfortable conversations with managers and higher-ups and learn to embrace the awkwardness. You'll be much better prepared for when it inevitably happens down the road.

✳ When you have frequent conversations with your boss about your career and money goals, nothing comes as a surprise.

Bet on Yourself, Not on Your Savings

Who better to talk money matters with than Jill Schlesinger, CFP and Emmy-nominated business analyst for CBS News?

Jill was comfortable with money from an early age—her father was a trader on the floor of the American Stock Exchange. As she watched him take massive risks as a trader, she also watched his investment life, which she described as "conservative, and pretty boring." Looking back, Jill thinks that her father set the tone for her approach to her career and her relationship with money, teaching her to take risks in her career while playing it safe with her cash.

Over the years, Jill learned that it was impossible to consistently "beat the market" over the long term, so she channeled most of her risk-taking energy into her career. She had started her career thinking she was going to be a commodities trader for the rest of her life, and truly, as one of eight women among eight hundred men, she loved it. Soon enough, she was ready for a change. She went from being a trader to being a wealth manager. It didn't feel like a risk to her, even though she was giving up giant piles of money to serve as a financial advisor. Similarly, when she jumped from being an advisor to being a media personality, she didn't feel like it was a huge risk, even though she could completely and publicly fail. Every time she was willing to consider an alternative to her current role somewhere, she was rewarded in her career, but with her money? She continued to simply save slowly, and invest in a very risk-averse fashion.

I was fascinated by someone who knows money better than most of us telling me to "take the career risks but don't take too many investment risks." Why one versus the other? Why not do both or neither? As Jill explained, "Your career is within your control. I'd rather take a risk that bets on my own human capital versus what's out of my control." (For the record, Jill also is a huge fan of entrepreneurship—because again, you're betting on yourself—but not so much in investing in other startups, or companies, in which you have no control.)

The bottom line? Take risks in your career, play it safe with your money.

JILL'S TIPS

* Take risks in your career but not with your investments.
* The best bet you can make is on yourself.

CHAPTER 5

Stand Out with Social Media

WHILE MONEY IS a tangible metric of success, perception is less black and white. And since we don't talk so much about money, perception quickly becomes reality. Today, there is no bigger shaper of perception than social media. I talk a lot about social media; after all, it's my day job. I help brands use social media to grow their businesses, and I'm pretty good at it. I wouldn't be good at it, though, if I didn't know how to use it for my own business, and for myself.

In 2008, the field of "social media marketing" was wide open. No one—and I mean, *no* one—knew what they were doing, least of all big behemoth brands. So when we got a call from the head of digital at Neutrogena, we weren't surprised, even though at that time we were an organization consisting of four people and a folding table in Queens, New York.

Man, Dave and I wanted this business bad. We didn't even care what they paid at the time; we just wanted to be able to say that our company worked with one of the largest skincare brands in the world. We wanted their logo on our Web site, and we were salivating. But we knew they already had about a thousand agencies, and we knew that since we were not a traditionally slick agency, we were at a big disadvantage. So we decided to use the tools that we would use for Neutrogena's success to our advantage—specifically, hyper-targeted Facebook ads.

We went into the ad platform and created an ad that we showed *only* to people who were interested in marketing, who worked at Neutrogena, and who lived in or around Los Angeles, where their U.S. corporate headquarters was located. We used an image of the bee that was once a part of our crudely designed logo and wrote the following copy: "We know how to reach you here, and we know how to reach your customers here, too. Thanks for reaching out and we're looking forward to working together."

The message was simple, and the result was instant. We received a call two days later, and without even pitching, we had won the business.

Now it's years later, and I'm building a podcast. I am looking to get in touch with high-powered decision makers to be on the show. What better place to reach these people than my favorite conversational network, Twitter? The thing about Twitter is, despite its being around a long time, it's underutilized for connecting with people. Since this is a business context, you'd think I'd reach out to guests on LinkedIn . . . but on Twitter, where everything is public, I can learn so much about a person, and add value to their lives before even reaching out. I'd start by retweeting articles they've written, or commenting on a show they're talking about. I'd eventually ask if they want to come on the show. My guest booking rate was 97 percent.

Of course, I have credibility on social media. In order to have credibility, you have to put in the work. But I would maintain that no matter *what* industry you work in, it's worth it to put the work in on social media to develop your personal brand.

Remember that whole section on "it's who you know"? Well, using social media, you really can know just about anybody. If you're an active participant, and your brand is reflected clearly when someone gives a quick glance at your profile, you are set up for success in a way that others aren't. And despite the fact that social media has become so mainstream, I would argue that very few people are putting in the work that can cut through the clutter to help achieve their goals.

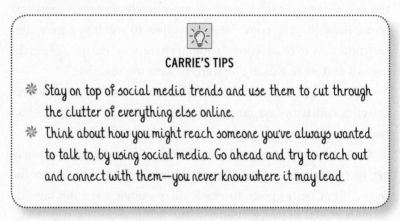

CARRIE'S TIPS

❋ Stay on top of social media trends and use them to cut through the clutter of everything else online.

❋ Think about how you might reach someone you've always wanted to talk to, by using social media. Go ahead and try to reach out and connect with them—you never know where it may lead.

Create Strong Connections Online and #IRL

If there's anyone who knows about how social media can get you ahead, it's Carmen Collins, who works on the Talent brand as a social media manager/lead at Cisco. Carmen has seen firsthand how social media can make a potential candidate infinitely more attractive.

Carmen and Casie Shimansky had connected via Twitter in the months leading up to Social Fresh Conference (thanks to the

#SocialFresh hashtag, they knew they'd both be attending) and a friendship had been formed, even though they'd never met in person. "It was a twiendship for the ages," says Carmen. "We were Twitter friends, working in the same industry, but I'd never formally met her IRL." (That, for all you non-millennials, means "in real life.")

When Carmen went to Social Fresh, she was super excited, not just to learn, but to meet others with her passion for social media. As she sat in the audience, she was next to a young woman who she saw was tweeting away. When the time came for networking, they turned to each other to say hi and made their discovery.

"Wait, you're @thenameisCasie?"

"Yes, and you're @cshirkeycollins!" (Gleeful giggles ensued.)

The online connection became a real-life relationship, and when Carmen had a job pop up on her WeAreCisco team, who do you think she hired? Casie.

Because Carmen works in the HR space within the social media world, I asked her about how important it is to "watch what you say" online. Turns out, Carmen doesn't shy away from applicants who have opinions, as long as they're smart about it.

"We tell our employees all the time to 'be themselves' in social media, and I think feeling strongly about things is okay—this includes more taboo topics like politics, too, by the way. The only thing I would warn is that I think an opinion needs to be addressed with civility and reason. If someone wouldn't hire you because they don't agree with your views, you don't want to work with them anyway. However, if someone wouldn't hire you because you trash-talk or call names or engage in uncivil liberties, they have not only a glimpse into your views, but your personality and how they would work with you. That's something, quite frankly, you should expect in this day and age of social media if you aren't smart about your presence."

CARMEN'S TIPS

❄ Take any positive relationship or connection that you have online, and think about how you might activate that relationship #IRL.

❄ Give as much as you get when forming relationships and friendships online—just like in the real world. Do something meaningful for an online connection today.

Be an Influencer

Social media is not just about the ability to form relationships, it's about the ability to create influence with your connections online as well. Just ask Brittany Hennessy, director, influencer talent at Hearst Digital Media.

Brittany started her career working at a traditional talent agency, but from the very beginning, she was working on her personal brand. She started a blog on the side. It was her "nightlife baby," a place where she covered all of the events she was attending thanks to her PR connections. When the blog took off, she quit her job to focus on it full-time. Brittany worked for several years as an influencer and was sent all around the globe, including a cruise with Rihanna.

Brittany then took her knowledge and set off to work for brands—showing each of them how to create their own influence and work with bloggers. She was highly sought after in the field, not only because she understood how it worked for the traditional "influencer" model you think of, but because she had actually put it into practice herself.

Throughout Brittany's entire career, she focused on her own social presence, which helped establish her credibility. When people googled Brittany Hennessy, they saw that she was credible, and influential, and creative—all because she continuously put effort into her personal brand. Ultimately, she landed her (originally unimaginable) dream job managing influencer campaigns for Hearst's digital properties. She now serves as an expert on the topic of influence at Hearst and digital conferences everywhere.

I asked Brittany if everyone should drop what they're doing and become an influencer. No, she said, but she does believe that everyone should worry about their personal brand online.

Brittany offered up a little experiment. Google yourself. If the first few things that pop up aren't your personal Web site/blog and your social media channels, you've got some work to do. If you are an active participant in the digital world, there is content attached to your name. If you're not creating that content, you're allowing the Internet, essentially a bunch of strangers, to tell your story to the world.

Another simple thing you can do today, Brittany says, is to purchase your name as a domain. "I own both my married name and my maiden name. If you don't have a lot of technical skills, a simple splash page with your photo, bio, and social handles will do the trick."

Brittany does see the opportunity for just about anyone to take their own personal brand and create a broader-scale level of influence.

"The majority of people on the Internet are curators—they're looking for content. This gives you a chance to create content that shows who you are and helps you get to the next level," says Brittany. The trick to that is mastering the concept of combined education and entertainment. Think about how you can create content that is of value to your audience, but also is entertaining. And,

Brittany says, "Be sure to weave in your own story. Make it personal."

You don't have to be a model or a makeup artist to be a social media influencer, either. There are influencers in every category—created simply by professionals who were determined to stand out. There's Dr. Zumin Damania, known to fans as ZDoggMD, who is a physician and uses comedy to demystify medical procedures. There's Cody Sperber, known as the Clever Investor, the person behind the most followed real estate investing account on Instagram, with over 400,000 followers. Name an industry, and chances are you can find an influencer in it who is building their business using social media.

Start by looking at your personal brand, says Brittany. But who knows? You could become the next influencer in your field.

BRITTANY'S TIPS

✳ Use social media personally so you will better understand how to use it professionally.
✳ Influence is valuable, no matter your career path. Invest some time in creating the perception you want of yourself by optimizing your public, searchable, social media profiles.

Own Your Online Brand

What if you have no idea where to start? And what if you don't want to use your social media for professional purposes? What if you just want to take pictures of your grilled cheese sandwich and comment on your friends' newsfeeds? Usually, when I'm stuck and something feels totally foreign to me, I reach deep into my arsenal and tap into my strongest reserves: my kids.

I always say if you want to know what's next in social media, ask a middle schooler. It turns out, they know a lot more than just "what's next." The children who have grown up in the age of the "Open Web" have a much greater understanding of personal brand and personal privacy than those of us who adopted social media as adults.

If you think about it, the millennials got screwed. Facebook came about when they were in college, and there were no rules about the social ramifications of Internet behavior. In their wildest dreams they couldn't imagine that the picture of them doing keg stands in their underwear would show up on the talent manager's computer screen and prevent them from getting their dream job.

Take Justine Sacco. As a thirty-year-old PR professional, she couldn't have imagined that a single ill-advised tweet sent to her 170 followers could ignite an international media firestorm that would cost her both her job and reputation.

Just before boarding the last leg of her long trip to Cape Town, she casually tweeted a joke, "Going to Africa. Hope I don't get AIDS. Just kidding, I'm white!"

When Justine boarded the plane, there were no replies to her tweet. When she landed eleven hours later, she was the #1 trending topic worldwide.

Twitter users were tracking her flight, waiting for her to land, and to see that not only had she lost her job, but she was a racist who needed to be destroyed. The hashtag #hasJustineLandedYet had death threats and more waiting for her. What had started as a thoughtless, casual joke written hastily turned into a serious lesson in social media etiquette for Justine and for all of us. Never mind that Justine's extended family in South Africa were African

National Congress supporters—the party of Nelson Mandela—and that Justine was active in supporting racial equality. All that mattered was that she'd made a bad racist-sounding joke that went viral.

As the character Erica Albright says in the film *The Social Network*: "The Internet's not written in pencil, Mark. It's written in ink."

Millennials were the first to learn this hard lesson. Generation Z? They're the ones working around it. Just ask my daughter Charlotte Kerpen, age fourteen.

Charlotte and her friends have a keen understanding of how people perceive you on social media. The trend toward "erasable media" messaging services like Snapchat, where messages disappear, is likely a direct result of the backlash from people who have had their lives affected by public gaffes on social media. Most social media usage for this generation takes place through messaging apps, where they communicate more privately with their friends, either in group chats or one-to-one erasable messages. But teens also have a keen understanding of their public social media image, too—and for that, there's currently one network that they use. That network? Instagram.

At first, I was confused when Charlotte told me about her "rinsta" and her "finsta"—aka her "real Instagram" and her "fake Instagram"—but after listening to her, it made all the sense in the world. Her "rinsta" is based on her full name and it is the picture of a perfect middle schooler. Every picture is bright and cheery. There are sunsets, there are cute shots with friends that look like a Gap ad, there is the perfectly crafted shot from her bat mitzvah. There are no more than nine photos on that profile at any time—photos get deleted when even more picture-perfect moments arise. If a college admissions guide went to search for Charlotte Kerpen on social media, they'd find a perfect vision of loveliness.

Then there's her "finsta." Charlotte's "finsta" features hundreds of Instagram posts, each more silly than the next. This is where she's documenting her life—and being as silly as can be. Of course, she's young, so her "finsta" is fairly tame. But the concept of a perfectly prepared personal brand handle, and a fake handle for more fun and flippant stuff—that's a concept that only a generation who witnessed the prior one's being vilified for their choices could make. As I looked at her friends on Instagram, I couldn't help but laugh at their "rinsta"/"finsta" names. There was Jocelyn—whose "finsta" was Joshie_Woshie_The_Floor. There was Laura, who frequently changed her name by season—and was currently in her FaLa.LaLa.Laura stage. Some friends had four to five "finsta"s, making them purposely difficult to find—avoiding parents and the public alike.

My favorite part about my conversation with Charlotte about social media was when I asked her about Facebook.

"Mom," she said, rolling her eyes at me. "Facebook is for old people."

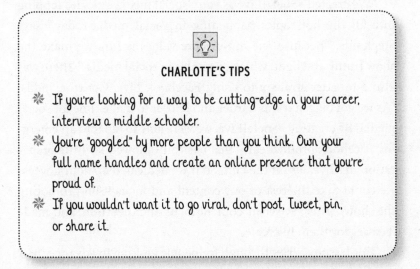

CHARLOTTE'S TIPS

❋ If you're looking for a way to be cutting-edge in your career, interview a middle schooler.

❋ You're "googled" by more people than you think. Own your full name handles and create an online presence that you're proud of.

❋ If you wouldn't want it to go viral, don't post, Tweet, pin, or share it.

Manage Your Social Media Schedule

While it somehow felt entirely natural to feature my daughter in this book, it felt funny to me that I would feature these next two ladies. Technically, they're competitors to my agency, Likeable Media. But since I served on the board of these two women's FAB PABs from their agency's beginning, I couldn't resist sharing their great stories. Stephanie Abrams Cartin and Courtney Spritzer are the cofounders of Socialfly, a boutique social media marketing and influencer agency. Their growth has been impressive—and one of the ways they've impressed me the most is by their early and effective use of Facebook Live.

Courtney and Stephanie both believe strongly in practicing what they preach . . . so they have to use social media pretty much constantly. You'll see them anywhere and everywhere. . . . but as their business grew, dedicating that time became increasingly more difficult. When the new format came out, they saw an opportunity to jump.

"We created #SocialLive as your 'social media quickie,' tapping into all the hot topics happening in social media today," says Stephanie. "Because one of our core values is fun, we make the show funny and light, which resonates in social media." There was also a broader strategy to using Facebook Live. Courtney adds, "As we got bigger, it was harder and harder to make time for social media. By creating #SocialLive, we were able to tap into an emerging Facebook product early that basically allowed for little preparation. It's live, it's off the cuff. So if we dedicated an hour a week, we could take the rest of our content and focus it on promoting the show." This gave their content focus and direction, and made it easier for them to create.

This lesson carries through for people looking to advance their careers, personal brands, and lives. By tapping into something simple, and building a strategy around that, you can have a multi-platform approach off of a single smart concept.

The result for Socialfly and my two favorite mentees? "Now, when clients find us, they almost always mention that they discovered us through our show or have watched our show before meeting us. It's instant credibility, and they already feel like they know us when we walk in the door."

STEPHANIE AND COURTNEY'S TIPS

❋ Social media can take a lot of time. Focus on the platforms and social media efforts that work within your schedule and that will be most effective or useful for you.

❋ Create a social media presence that helps people feel like they know you before they've even met you.

CUT THE CRAP AND GET THINGS DONE:
A CASE STUDY WITH JUSTICE PAT DI MANGO

 For this case study, I wanted to focus on a woman I know personally—someone who can "work it" more efficiently than anyone I know—Justice Pat Di Mango. In the 1980s, my father was a State Supreme Court justice in Brooklyn, New York. I often used to go sit in his chambers, just to hang out with his fabulous, glamorous law clerk, Pat Di Mango. She was Mona Lisa Vito on steroids—the quintessential Italian Brooklynite—smart as a whip, perfectly put together, and she was everything I wanted to be and more.

Pat and I formed a special connection, and I've followed her in her career ever since. It was evident even then that she was going places—so it was no surprise when I opened *The New York Times* to see that my father's former law clerk, who had become one of the most successful judges in Brooklyn and the Bronx, was hand selected by Judge Judith Sheindlin (aka Judge Judy) to star on the new hit show *Hot Bench*.

Pat recognized the benefits of a no-bull attitude in her career very early on. Right after law school, she landed a job as an assistant district attorney in Brooklyn. At a time when assistant district attorneys could take weeks to settle one case, Pat was somehow able to get people through the courts without the same levels of bureaucracy that others did.

That's when she met my father, Judge Steven Fisher. Pat knew that becoming a law clerk for my father would be a perfect next career move in order to achieve her ultimate goal of becoming a judge. She decided to apply. At the interview, Pat told Judge Fisher about her love of navigating the court system—of schmoozing the right people to get the job done. Fortunately, he told her, he loved to write, and was not a big fan of the schmooze. He hired her, and a brilliant partnership was formed.

After ten years as a law clerk, Pat became a judge, and quickly became known for two things—moving through cases quickly, and extracting the truth from the most dishonest of criminals.

And one thing that made her different from other judges? She kept a phone right next to her on the bench.

"I'd be staring at a kid who said he was in school and couldn't possibly have committed the crime he was accused of. I'd say to him, 'I tell you what, you can tell me the truth right now, or I can call the school and verify that you were there. If you tell me the truth now, I'll let you off easy. If you don't, and I check with the school and you're lying, there's going to be a problem.' He'd look at me straight in the face and say, 'Go ahead, call!' I would call the school and they'd say, 'Oh, that kid? He hasn't been here for months.' People who grow up in an environment where lying is a constant thing don't even know they're lying anymore. I'd call them on it, no problem."

The phone that Judge Di Mango had with her proved to be handy in much more than just checking up on defendants' alibis—it helped her move through cases quickly. "I would do everything in the moment," she said. "There was no adjourning of court to wait and see. I'd get it done right then and there."

Pat's no-nonsense attitude served her well. Her courtroom was no longer just filled with legal teams. Crowds would form, watching her work. Her success and her speed were so widely recognized, she was asked to go from Brooklyn to the Bronx, and clean up the huge backlog of cases there. Pat left the comforts of Brooklyn for the Bronx.

In the Bronx, defendants would languish in jail for months—and often years—before they would complete a trial. In a year, Pat was able to negotiate hundreds of plea bargains, doing what no other judge in the Bronx could—closing stalled cases in real time. She reduced the backlog by 50 percent in less than a year.

As the awareness of Pat's style grew, so did the audiences who watched her. Some were more interesting than others—including some producers. Pat was sitting at home in her sweatpants when her phone rang. It was the office of Judge Judy.

Pat was flabbergasted. Judge Judy, television personality and the world's most famous judge, was interested in finding a judge who was just like her, but younger, to fill a role on the upcoming show she was producing called *Hot Bench*. One of her connections in New York had been watching Pat clean up the Bronx—and Judge Judy was interested in bringing Pat on board.

On the phone, Judy asked Pat to come out on Thursday to Los Angeles to audition. Pat was overwhelmed. "I'm really busy. I have cases on Thursday! I'm cleaning up the Bronx!"

"Okay," said Judge Judy, "Friday it is."

(Clearly, Judge Judy believed in cutting the crap, too.)

Now, splitting her time between Los Angeles and New York, Pat is in an entirely new career—that of a true "celebrity judge." On *Hot Bench*, she's the same person she's always been—calling defendants on their bluffs, and getting the answers she needs to get to the heart of the matter. And she's having the time of her life.

In this section, we talked about how to "work it professionally." For Pat, that means being honest, direct, straightforward, and quintessentially herself. So what's the lesson to take away from her story? Cut the crap and be yourself and you'll find your own path to success.

Okay, it's official. We've learned how to build the network of our dreams, and how to seek advice from the fabulous women around us. We've learned how to work that network and get the jobs of our dreams, all while making money in the process. And finally, we've learned how social media can both help and hurt our careers—and how to "work it" to our advantage. These are the basics—the things we need to have a successful and meaningful career. But there are the things that we need, and the things that we want. And sometimes, figuring out exactly what you want out of your career and life takes practice. It's time to head on over to part 2, where we learn how to "work it passionately."

PART 2

Work It Passionately

CHAPTER 6

Yes, No, Maybe So—A Guide to Intuition

I F I HAD to offer one word that summed up what you needed to do to truly "work it," that word would be *instinct*. Knowing how to recognize what you really want by channeling your gut instincts is a learned skill—and once you master it, you'll be able to make critical life and career decisions much faster. Over the next three chapters, you'll read about important decisions that women faced—and how they decided what to do by focusing on their gut instincts.

One of my earliest critical decisions was around where to finish my college education. At the end of my sophomore year, I went through a really bad breakup. I was living in Boston, attending Emerson College, when my life started to fall apart. I decided to move home to New York in my junior year to try to make my toxic relationship work, and when it didn't, I ended up sitting in a therapist's office for the first time in my life. My hair was short and bleached blond, I had gained a ton of weight—and I felt like a completely different person walking into that office. I didn't even know myself.

As I sat across from the therapist and talked to her, our conversations felt like a gift from God. She was able to help me work through my feelings around the breakup, about the changes I'd undergone, and my feelings about myself, all at once. Slowly, I started feeling better, but I was still living at home and felt like my life had made a huge detour. Now I was officially healthy, yet still lost.

My therapist suggested an exercise that she called the "Animal of Influence." I was asked to sit still as she guided me through a meditation exercise where I would wait for an animal to appear. I was never good at meditation, and pretty skeptical of this stuff, but I tried it. Almost immediately, I saw an owl.

She asked me what the owl was doing, where it was, what it looked like. The owl was soaring over the Boston city skyline. It was peaceful, flying with a quiet confidence. Suddenly I knew I needed to go back to Boston and return to Emerson College. About a month later, that's exactly what I did. (Oh, and because I was twenty and still pretty stupid, I stopped on my drive up and got a tattoo of an owl. I'm not a tattoo person, btw.) Going back to Boston was a humbling, hard decision—I had left my friends, my school that I loved, all to follow a boy. I felt embarrassed and humiliated. But once I was back there, it became clear that following my gut and coming back to school was one of the best decisions of my life. And it was all thanks to my therapist and the owl—who now rests on my back, reminding me constantly of the importance of following your gut.

(Note to my daughters: If you're visited by an animal of influence, and it helps you make an important decision—buy a pretty necklace with said animal's imagery. No need for permanent ink on your body, unless you're *really* into that sort of thing, which your mother was not when she got her own "trendy tribal owl.")

Years later, I was speaking at WomanCon, an event for female leaders and entrepreneurs. There was a session on visioning, and since I hate to speak at a conference without attending at least some of the conference itself, I hopped in with my colleague. Again there was a guided meditation, except this time the woman asked us to envision ourselves knocking on the door of our home five years from now. And the person who answers the door? You guessed it, you. Five years later. She asked what we looked like, what we were wearing, what we were doing at that time.

I saw myself in my home, holding a small boy. I was wearing hippie-dippie flowy clothes, and I had built and sold a successful agency. In the conversation with myself, I told myself to never be unappreciative of my willingness to slow down—even if I wasn't as fast as competitors who outpaced me in business, I was creating the life I wanted on the terms I wanted. When I finished, I felt like the exercise was pretty dead-on. About a week later, I took a pregnancy test, and there was the boy I was envisioning during the exercise.

CARRIE'S TIPS

❋ When you're unsure of what you want, consider trying meditation and/or vision exercises that can often give you clarity on what you're looking to accomplish.

❋ When in doubt, go with your gut. It usually won't let you down.

Be Your Own Advisor

Sometimes, identifying what you want is not about taking time out to connect with yourself. Sometimes it's about insights from others that may or may not be reflective of what you truly want.

Laurie Seidman was a producer on the TV series *Medium* when her gut first started to sound the alarms. It might have been because she was looking at all of her mentors, seeing them in their late fifties and sixties, working on the set, on their feet, for upward of eighty hours a week. Laurie's gut told her that producing could not be a longer-term goal; when she closed her eyes and saw herself at fifty years old, it simply wasn't what she saw. Laurie had to find a plan B—and since *Medium* was wrapping up in just a few months, Laurie had some time to think.

Laurie thought about becoming a creative executive at a network, which would fulfill her creative vision and give her more of the lifestyle she wanted. She activated her network, reaching out to set up fifteen-minute meetings with everyone she'd helped over the years as a producer, or anyone she simply had a great relationship with. She did a few things at each meeting. First, she expressed her desire to transition to another area of the business. Second, she told each person that she wanted to see what they thought her experience lent itself to, and what they thought would be the right next step for her to transition to. Third, she thanked them and asked if there was anyone else they thought she could or should meet with to help her figure out the transition.

In the course of a year, Laurie had seventy meetings.

Of the seventy meetings that Laurie had, not one of them recommended that she go onto the network executive side. "They all said something to the effect of—you are a creative person—a producer—you would hate working at the network. You need to be with creative people and close to a production. Most liked studio production for me," Laurie said. The stigma around network executives is that they're out of touch—stuck in an office. They thought for sure she'd be bored.

When a former studio executive from *Medium* called her and said that while he didn't have an executive position at the studio for prime-time scripted television, he did know of a network executive position in daytime, Laurie was not enthusiastic about it. After all the feedback, she was downright scared. But she knew there were only going to be so many opportunities to transition out of her current area and create the life she wanted for herself. Her gut was telling her—take the interview.

Laurie was impressed by the woman she was meeting with. She loved the energy and vision of the person leading daytime. After she left the interview, she closed her eyes and tried to get to how she was really feeling. She recalled growing up watching soap operas and daytime television and felt a deep connection.

Laurie got the job and was no longer afraid. She was actually thrilled. And it turns out, it was the best decision she ever made. Now an executive of daytime network television for over five years, Laurie says that decision, and not listening to her seventy advisors, changed her life for the better.

Laurie found that not only was the job *very* creative, it allowed her to see things from a higher perspective. "I'm not just focused on the day-to-day; I'm focused on the bigger picture: the week-to-week, the month-to-month, the year-to-year." And Laurie doesn't find herself trapped in an office at all. "Actually, a lot of the time, I'm on the set of my shows." All of that, simply from listening to the voice that mattered most—her own.

LAURIE'S TIPS

❈ Sometimes the only advisor you need to listen to is yourself.

❈ Look at people who are twenty years ahead of you on your career trajectory. Do you like how their careers have turned out? Are they where you want to be one day?

Careers Don't Have to Be Conventional

In my case and in Laurie's case, it took a little time and reassurance to connect with our instincts. In what is perhaps the most unconventional career and family story based entirely on gut, I'd like to introduce you to Claire Díaz-Ortiz.

Claire was always on the fast track, and often took on too much. When she completed her undergrad and master's degrees in just four years at Stanford, she was left feeling totally burned out.

Claire took a year off, living in a Mexican village that she'd read about in a book—a place where middle-aged people went to retire. (Never mind that she wasn't yet middle-aged—she simply needed a break.) After she was reenergized, she still wasn't sure what she wanted to do, so she and a college friend decided to take a nine-month trip around the world.

They also decided to start a travel blog, which picked up a following as they trekked across the globe. Their last stop was Kenya, where they were going to climb Mount Kenya. It was recommended that they stay at a guesthouse at the base of the mountain, which was part of an orphanage.

Claire was hesitant. She was uncomfortable with the thought

of staying at an orphanage, but when she arrived and had lunch with the elders who ran the orphanage, she had a defining moment. "I remember I stepped out to go to the restroom, and a feeling just came over me that this was exactly where I need to be, and that this was the start of the next chapter of my life." Both Claire and her friend decided to stay for the next year, and the elders asked them to start a running club with the orphans.

From day one of Claire's stay at the orphanage, she connected with a boy named Sammy. He was thirteen, but he was small for his age. "He looked like he was seven, and was so smart—talking about then-Senator Barack Obama—such a brilliant kid." Claire was very impressed. Claire and Sammy became very close. She became focused on how she could get Sammy to the States. Claire was twenty-five at the time, and there was no legal way to adopt him; she was simply too young. Claire begged her parents to adopt Sammy, but they were unwilling to commit at that time. Claire continued to work on her plans for Sammy, and formed a nonprofit called Hope Runs, based on a philanthropic running club, all while writing her blog, which continued to gain momentum.

After a year in Kenya, Claire wanted to get an MBA to help give her the education needed to grow her nonprofit. She applied and received a scholarship to Oxford in 2008. A founder of an up-and-coming startup came to speak at Oxford; his name was Biz Stone, and his startup was Twitter. After the speech, Claire approached him. She wanted to mix the tech world with social action. Biz offered her an internship in San Francisco to increase her understanding of how Twitter might be able to help with social impact. She became one of the first employees, and many noticed her incredible work for good. In fact, she was known as the "woman who got the Pope on Twitter!"

She was having great success, although Sammy was still on her mind the whole time. She continued to visit him regularly while constantly searching for solutions to get Sammy the opportunity he deserved. After much research, Claire was able to assume legal guardianship for Sammy, getting him a full ride at a boarding school in Maine.

During the next six years at Twitter, Claire continued to grow her career while Sammy attended high school and spent a year in Ecuador as part of the Global Citizen Year program. Claire was thrilled to see him have such amazing experiences, and she was happy to see her own career flourishing. Sammy and Claire decided that they needed to share their story, so they wrote and published a book, *Hope Runs: An American Tourist, a Kenyan Boy, a Journey of Redemption*. When Sammy decided to attend college and ultimately work for a nonprofit in Kenya, Claire was incredibly proud of his choice.

Claire made the decision to leave her dream job. The reason? Family. Claire had met her husband, José, when she was on a brief stop during her travels in Buenos Aires before attending Oxford. For much of her time at Twitter she truly felt spread across three continents—her career was in San Francisco, her husband was in Argentina, and her foster son was in Kenya. With Sammy now studying in Kenya, Claire got pregnant with her daughter, and she and José thought long and hard about where they wanted to live. The answer was Argentina.

Claire resigned from Twitter shortly after her daughter was born, and began her career as a writer and consultant. She went on to give birth to twins. Claire can't imagine going back to a corporate job now, since the time with her family is the most important thing in her life, and she's able to earn enough to live happily in the place she loves.

> **CLAIRE'S TIPS**
> * When a strong feeling or desire comes over you, rather than fighting it, see where it might take you.
> * When you abandon a traditional career path and its expectations, you open up a whole new world of possibilities.

The Secret to Insight? Trust.

Although Barbara Corcoran didn't have *quite* as unconventional a path as Claire did, her ability to identify her instincts and call it like she sees it is rather unusual. I remember being in awe of Barbara Corcoran long before her days as an investor on *Shark Tank*. To me, she was best known as an icon of New York real estate—particularly because she was written about everywhere I looked.

Barbara was a PR machine—and I remember hearing her speak at a conference I attended. Decked out in her standard bright yellow attire, Barbara talked about how she mailed *The New York Times* a "Corcoran Report" about celebrity home listings—and how they picked it up as news. Her chutzpah always astounded me, and I was in awe of her as a business icon. So I wasn't surprised when she appeared on *Shark Tank* and emerged as an entertainment star as well as an investment tycoon.

I asked Barbara about her gut; it was so evident from her *Shark Tank* appearances that her gut was what drove her with regard to investments. On television, it appeared as if she instantly knew whether an investment was right for her, and I wanted to tap into that decision-making ability. It turns out, Barbara's gut guided her long before her days in the tank.

Barbara recalls when she trusted one of the biggest developers in town using simply a handshake. "There wasn't a person in this town that didn't think I was crazy—they were sure that he would rip me off." She was asked time and time again how she could involve her time, money, and staff in work that was based on the words "trust me" and a handshake.

The answer? Barbara believed strongly in her gut. When the deal worked and worked big, she loved telling everyone, "Hey, guess what? You were wrong."

Barbara also tells the story of when she first met her now infamous ex-boyfriend Ramon Simone in the diner where she worked as a waitress in New Jersey. He took one look at her and said, "A smart girl like you should really live in New York City." Barbara felt that advice in the core of her gut, and that night quit her job and moved to New York City.

And sometimes when Barbara trusted her gut, it was against the most formidable of opponents. One of those opponents? Her mother. Two years after her move to New York City, she decided to start her own business. Her mother said, "Barbara, you have had twenty-two jobs and you're twenty-three years old. You hop around way too much. Build your résumé and wait two years, please." Looking back, Barbara is certain of one thing. "If I had waited two more years, I never would have started." Barbara set out on her own and the rest was history.

Barbara looks back on her entire career and can honestly say her gut has never steered her wrong. It may be because of her litmus test that tests her gut against her most valuable asset of all: her children.

Barbara has a twenty-four-year-old son and an eleven-year-old daughter. Before any decision around trusting someone, she asks herself the following question:

"If there was a war, and I had to hand my kids over to these
people, could I come back to them in ten years and
my children would be okay?"

The answer is never gray—it's yes or no. And that's how she knows whether or not she can trust someone. "If you think about it, in business deals, you're raising a kid together and you have to trust each other completely. You can build tremendous strength from people if you trust them." Barbara cites the example of the only partner she's ever worked with for ten years. That partner wrote all of the checks and Barbara trusted her implicitly. "Look, she could have easily ripped me off. But she didn't. I have a good sense of who to work with. And that's never steered me wrong."

BARBARA'S TIPS

※ Having good insight is all about trust—go with your gut until it proves you wrong, but trust that it will prove you right. If you end up being wrong, examine why. I bet you ignored something that your gut was telling you in the first place.

※ Ask yourself if you'd make this same decision in an emergency situation. If you made the decision abruptly and left for a while, what would the result be when you came back?

CHAPTER 7

Say Yes to the Mess

I HAVE A PROBLEM that I've been working on for most of my adult life. I say yes. A lot. In fact, when I read Shonda Rhimes's *Year of Yes*, I felt like I needed a book called *The Year of No Freaking Way*. I always take the coffee meeting. I allow people to just "pick my brain" for a few minutes. I attend every house party where my friends sell various makeup/pots and pans/skincare regimens. I say yes, a lot, even when I don't want to. I like the feeling of helping others. It's hard for me to stop, even when it's to my own detriment. Over time, I've learned to curb this bad habit. But sometimes saying yes is *exactly* what we need to do for our careers.

I was on maternity leave with my third child, Seth, when I attended a playgroup that a friend asked me to join. Newsflash: I hate mommy playgroups. First of all, if you remember, I am the extroverted introvert, so I will spend the entire time talking to every mom while secretly feeling like a nervous wreck. Second, Seth is my third child, and is twelve years younger than my daughter

Charlotte and eight years younger than my daughter Kate. I already went through the horribly awkward process of mommy-friending, and I had my crew. I didn't need new friends. But, of course, someone asked me to go, so off I went.

Seth was a very mushy baby. He was not quick to roll over, or sit up, or crawl, or walk, even. He much preferred snuggling in my arms and reading books as a baby—which I will be forever grateful for in retrospect. At the time, however, it caused me great worry. And playdates, when you're sitting next to other children the same age as your baby, cause you to compare.

> *"Oh, is he sitting yet?"*
> *"Oh, he takes a pacifier, huh?"*
> *"Wow, he's in 2T clothes already?"*

The list goes on. So anyway, needless to say I was filled with dread as I walked through the door. And there I saw her. Sitting in the corner with her baby who looked exactly like Seth, there was my new mom friend. I sat down next to her.

"Seth isn't rolling yet."

"Oh please," she said. "Bennett is so giant he couldn't roll if he tried. I can't even believe you can get Seth's thighs into jeans. I'm jealous."

Our friendship was formed. She was a principal of a middle school, and was also on maternity leave. We were both very busy, but we did manage to get together every once in a while, and I felt really lucky to have her as a friend. One day, toward the last week of my maternity leave, she texted me.

"Carrie, I know you work on social media stuff. I need to do something for my PTA around digital safety for parents and teens. Will you come to my PTA meeting and present?"

Let me just level set for you about where I am in my life at this point. I am now the CEO of a multimillion-dollar global agency. I have three children—one of whom was pushed out of me fairly recently. I have many other responsibilities, including helping to care for a mother with multiple sclerosis, and a writing and speaking career that has recently taken off. I have exactly zero hours of free time, and PTA meetings are usually in the evening, which is my special "no phone zone" kid time. I do, however, think parents and children need to have more conversations about their social media usage, and I did think I could help.

"I'm in. Time and date?"

I frantically start planning my "Parenting in a Digital Age" presentation. I've never done it before, so it's a "build from scratch" type of operation. Since I have no time during the day, I'm building this post–"no phone zone," after the kids are asleep.

This, of course, leaves me open to advice from my number one fan and protector of my time, Mr. Dave Kerpen. He gives me the *oh no, not again* look and begs me to cancel. Much to his dismay, I press on.

On the last evening of my maternity leave, I go to the Lakeside Elementary School all the way across Long Island to deliver my presentation, which is based on the premise that parents need to learn how to use social media in order to better understand how their children are using it. It's a mix of fact and fun, and I spend a good amount of time teaching moms how to vomit rainbows on Snapchat.

One mom in particular approaches me afterward.

"Can I have your card? I am in procurement at Johnson and Johnson, in charge of our global agency services. I think you should do this presentation for our marketing team. We are all marketers, but we're at a loss as to how to deal with the challenges of parenting in a digital age."

What do you think I said to that one?

HELL YES.

Johnson & Johnson is a Fortune 500 company that agencies throughout the world would kill to work with. And I ended up getting in there all from saying yes to a mom from a playgroup I didn't even want to attend.

Of course, I have lots of stories that didn't turn out the same way. The magical J&J story was one where I put myself out there without trying to win business—it was the most random of random acts. And because I don't want you to have total magical thinking about my business mojo, I'll tell you this story, too.

Right before I got pregnant with Seth, I met an amazing woman who worked at Procter & Gamble, the *other* Fortune 500 that agencies trip over themselves to work with. She took a liking to me, and asked if I could keynote their women's conference the following spring. I was overjoyed.

When I got pregnant with Seth, I knew that I would be about thirty-five weeks along at the time of the conference. I called her and let her know I was still willing to do it if they were willing to take the risk that my getting there was not guaranteed. (They are in Cincinnati, and I am in New York.) Provided I didn't go into labor early, I was still legally allowed to fly, so what could go wrong? My contact said let's go for it, and I did.

It was a snowy Tuesday in March when I flew out to Cincy, in a fabulous print maternity dress, ready to win big. I delivered the speech of a lifetime. I poured my heart and soul into it, and the room of three hundred women laughed, cried, and rose to their feet. It felt totally worth it.

Our flight home was cancelled due to weather, and my colleague and I were stranded overnight. We managed to board a packed plane that had mechanical issues, and then were deplaned and rerouted through a multiple-stop route. I ignored the contractions I was feeling intermittently throughout, and just prayed. We arrived home safely.

After the speech, I followed up with the marketing contacts I met. One by one, they left P&G. Every contact I had met seemed to have either left or moved out of marketing, including my initial contact who was so incredible.

I was certain I would get business from that trip. When I didn't, I felt like a huge failure. But not every yes is going to be a fairy tale, and you have to be prepared to take the good with the bad. The point is, it's worth it to say yes to the mess. In the end, your yeses will always sort themselves out.

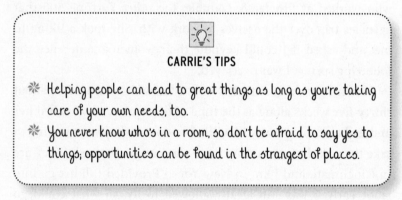

CARRIE'S TIPS

❋ Helping people can lead to great things as long as you're taking care of your own needs, too.

❋ You never know who's in a room, so don't be afraid to say yes to things; opportunities can be found in the strangest of places.

How to Define Your Own Job

Sometimes, the path you should take isn't clear—but the decision to travel on that path feels as clear as can be.

Linda Boff was the chief marketing officer at iVillage, a media company with Web sites targeted at women. She decided she was ready to move on, but wanted to make sure she found the right opportunity. Linda was approached by Beth Comstock, then the chief marketing officer at GE, with a position that Linda describes as the "grayest, most opaque job description" that she'd ever seen. She was asked to come on board and "think about digital at GE." The job didn't even sit in the brand or advertising department—and she'd have no staff. Plus, plenty of people at GE had some form of digital in their job descriptions. She'd have little to no resources, and a potential political land mine. All she had to go on was that they were "looking for new ways to think about our brand." Linda was the CMO of a $100 million digital company with a clearly defined role. What was the upside of this new role?

Linda ended up taking the job. She took a complete leap of faith because, she says, "Ultimately, it's about the people." Linda had faith in Beth and her vision for the company, and it didn't hurt that she had worked at GE before and loved the culture. She looked at the job as an opportunity to reinvent herself and the digital footprint of GE. And that's exactly what she did.

Now at GE for over twelve years, Linda Boff was promoted to the CMO position in 2015, and is largely credited for GE's transformation to a digital-first brand. Looking back, Linda says that taking that "grayest, most opaque job" was one of the single best career decisions she's ever made.

LINDA'S TIPS

※ Choose wisely. Who you work for is just as important as what you do.

※ A job opportunity doesn't have to be presented perfectly. If you're bold, you can have a hand in forming it into your dream role.

The Harder the Yes, the Bigger the Payoff

Sometimes the decision to say yes doesn't come easily. Such is the case with Ebony's Power 100 winner and CMO of American Family Insurance, Telisa Yancy.

Telisa recalls two times that she made gutsy "yes" moves that were challenging. The first was leaving a job that she knew wasn't right for her, and the second was leaving her sexy career path working with one of the world's biggest consumer brands to work for an insurance company.

Telisa was always a brand marketer at heart. As a child, she remembers sitting in front of the television, watching the iconic Coke commercials, and thinking, *I want to do that!* Intensely focused on achieving her dreams, Telisa landed her first job at Ford Motor Company straight out of college. She spent the next five years at Ford in several different positions, learning the ins and outs of general management, marketing, operations, and sales. Telisa lived and breathed the brand and they thoroughly supported her in return, sending her to business school and investing in her. Telisa eventually wanted to spread her wings outside of the automotive category. She decided to go to another seemingly exciting brand, Burger King.

From the moment Telisa arrived, she knew that the Burger King job wasn't a fit. She made a really gutsy decision very early in her tenure there—she said "yes" to saying "no, thank you" and left Burger King with less than a year under her belt.

When Telisa saw the posting for American Family Insurance, she almost didn't take the interview. Although AmFam is a Fortune 300, it didn't have the typical sex appeal that Burger King or Ford might for marketers. Also, the role had a director title, and when Telisa left Burger King, she was at a vice president level.

With another large offer from a telecom company with a lot of "sizzle," Telisa was going to skip the interview. She spoke to her husband.

"Telisa," he said. "You know I think you're brilliant and can do anything. You've told me for years that you wanted to make an impact. Why would you take a job where you're basically encouraging people to use their phones more when you could use your powers to help people protect themselves?"

This was the first lightbulb moment for Telisa. She took the interview and saw she'd be working for a powerful female leader for whom she had immense respect. It turns out, this was the push she needed to make the counterintuitive decision to say yes to this job.

That's not to say it was easy. Telisa was a very different kind of marketer than insurance firms might be used to. "I was surrounded by people with degrees in math—it was a very different environment. It did take some adjustment, but in the end, it also allowed me to make a tremendous impact."

It turns out Telisa saw an opportunity at this Fortune 300 company to make an impact not just for the customers, but for the employees and the community that they serve. The result of this yes? Telisa grew into the Chief Marketing Officer position, and reshaped the brand to have massive meaning. "This was a time where insurance companies were focused on creating campaigns based on humor, mascots, and commoditization of price. This didn't match with what I was seeing for insurance. When you achieve something, you secure it with insurance so you can go onto your next big accomplishment without worry. It all traces back to the American Dream—the idea that with hard work, dedication, and optimism we can achieve whatever we set our minds to. That's a mission with impact."

TELISA'S TIPS

❋ If you know that something's not a fit, get out as soon as you can. Don't be afraid to quit; sometimes it's the right option.

❋ The harder it is to say yes to something, the greater the payoff will be when it works.

Passion Is a Calling—Answer the Call

If you had asked six-year-old Randi Zuckerberg what her life's dream was, she would have told you that she was going to live in New York and be involved in theater—likely singing on Broadway. She always had a very sure sense of who she was and what she wanted to do—an unusual trait to find in a kid. So when Randi woke up in her early thirties, living in California and working in technology, she thought to herself, *What happened here?*

Sure, her life was wonderful. She was married and had her first child, and had found herself with a seat at the table at Facebook, after joining the company that was once an idea in her brother Mark's college dorm room. Randi was unequivocally passionate about her job at Facebook. Yet something was nagging at her. Her dreams—the part of her that had made her so sure of who she was as a person—had taken a backseat.

In Silicon Valley, says Randi, there is no room for outside passions or side projects. "It's a unique culture—you're supposed to be singularly focused on the tech company you are working for. If you're not, you're not considered serious, and therefore, you're not taken seriously." There's also a double standard for women in particular. "They're already thinking you can be distracted because you might be considering having children." For Randi, having a hobby or a passion outside of work seemed too "luxurious." And at the time she was loving her career, so it was worth the trade-off. Having the opportunity to be at a high-growth company like Facebook and being on the front lines there was worth it. Of course, until it wasn't.

"You get to a point in your life where there is no amount of money or power or prestige in your career that is worth giving up what you're passionate about." And for Randi Zuckerberg that was on a random Thursday, at age thirty-two.

She was sitting in her living room in Silicon Valley when she got a call from a producer of a Broadway show called *Rock of Ages*. The show had been running on Broadway for five years, and they wanted to shake it up a bit and bring in some new audiences. Specifically, *Rock of Ages* was looking for someone in the tech industry who could bring a new audience to Broadway. The producer had spoken to several people who had mentioned Randi—and they were calling to offer her a leading role on Broadway.

It had been ten years. Ten years of giving up her dream of being in theater to pursue a new life in tech—and suddenly, her dream had found her. She was absolutely positive that she was being punked. "I'll get right back to you," she said.

Randi put down the phone and called every mentor she had. She was surprised to hear that many of them thought it was a big mistake. "They said to me, if you do this—you will not be taken seriously in business ever again." Randi talks of the single identity syndrome. "As a woman, people only like you to have one identity. You can't be a tech entrepreneur and in the arts. That just doesn't fly."

The one "mentor" who was most in favor of the jump? Randi's husband, Brent. He knew it was all she'd ever really wanted to do, and he offered to play single dad while she took the gig, and fly up on weekends to watch her perform. That was the push she needed.

Randi moved to New York the following Monday, just five days after she was offered the role. That same Monday, Randi made a key discovery. She was pregnant with her second child. Randi was slated to be in the show four months from beginning rehearsals. "Did I mention I'd be wearing a glitter leotard?" she said. Randi let them know and did what anyone pursuing their dream would do: "I can learn the role in two weeks," she said. Two weeks later, Randi opened as Regina on Broadway. Randi did over thirty performances of *Rock of Ages*—only leaving as her pregnancy was starting to show.

When Randi's husband, Brent, came to see the show, he helped reflect what Randi was feeling. "He said to me, 'Randi, this is the happiest and lightest I've ever seen you. We are moving to New York.'" His support made it easy. He had been building his own career and was willing to trade that all in to help her in her dream. How could she possibly say no?

Randi's life is now exactly what Silicon Valley wouldn't accept—it's three-dimensional. She's an entrepreneur, and she's devoted to the arts. As an entrepreneur, she's an investor, and runs a media company. As a patron of the arts, she now sits on the board of the American Theatre Wing, which votes on the Tony Awards. She actually sees three to four shows per week, running her business during the day, tucking the kids into bed and heading out to the theater. She's also joined the board of Lincoln Center, and invested in the hit Broadway show *Dear Evan Hansen*. Even though she's not singing onstage all the time, she feels like she has been able to marry the two loves of her life—using her entrepreneurial spirit and bringing it to the arts.

Looking back now, Randi can't believe she almost got talked

out of it. "It made me think about how many women are out there, shelving parts of their passion and identity to please people who will never, ever be pleased by them anyway. Maybe it confuses people, or upsets them, that my life isn't in a little box—and that I'm not a hundred percent in technology and have a more three-dimensional career path. I say, so what?"

Randi is quick to point out that following your passion is important, but you also need to ensure that whatever you do can be built into a career. "I'm not saying to everyone, 'Go abandon everything and chase your dreams,' and certainly not if it's not practical. But I am not an advocate for anyone being stuck in their career, either. Earning money and building a career for yourself as a woman is essential, because it gives you a lot of power and decision-making in your life. But figuring out what you truly like and not ignoring that part of you is important."

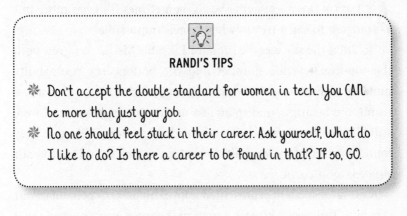

RANDI'S TIPS

* Don't accept the double standard for women in tech. You CAN be more than just your job.
* No one should feel stuck in their career. Ask yourself, What do I like to do? Is there a career to be found in that? If so, GO.

CHAPTER 8

Learn to Love the No

As important as saying yes is, sometimes it's even more important to say no, even when it feels impossible.

In 2016, the sky was the limit for Likeable Media. We grew both the top-line revenue number *and* the bottom-line profitability number simultaneously, which is tough to do. It means that we won more business, and spent less to run that business, and were still filled with satisfied clients who didn't just find us likeable, they found us pretty darn loveable. Except for, as luck would have it, our single largest client.

Our largest client represented approximately 25 percent of our revenue. This was a bizarre situation, because every obstacle that usually dooms a client/agency relationship had happened here, and we had it work to our advantage. First, the company merged with another company, and we had to fight for the business against the agency that was handling the acquirer. We won the whole shebang.

Then a new CMO was put in place, which is the single biggest reason agencies get fired: CMOs have their own agenda and their own relationships and need to make an impact quickly with those. But we managed to gain her trust.

Suddenly, a new VP of marketing came in like a bull in a china shop—he was obsessed with big-name agencies and we were a small independent. We had to work hard to win his heart, but we did, with our great work and our vision for where the brand could go. He gave us even more business, and we temporarily stepped up to act in lieu of their entire digital marketing team while he searched for the right people to work underneath him.

When they needed a head of social media to serve as our agency contact and to head up their digital social efforts, I tapped a former VP from my agency who was ready to take on a new challenge, and referred her to the job. I breathed a sigh of relief. With the two senior key relationships solidified, and my "person" being placed in the day-to-day role, I was golden.

As the client contacts changed, so did their direction. It went up, it went down, it went all around. While we were focused on using social media to generate revenue for them, they wanted "award-winning creative that was cool." Defining cool became a bigger and bigger challenge. The CMO's cool was different from the VP's cool—and our day-to-day contact seemed to be in the middle, wanting to make her own unique mark. Suddenly, despite our relationship building, we were not new, shiny, or "cool" for this client.

So when the VP called to tell me they'd like to RFP the business—that we'd done nothing wrong, that we'd done great work, and we'd gotten them better results than they'd ever had—I was only half-surprised. They wanted to see "what else was out there"—and he said I had a great shot to retain the business, especially since I knew them so well. I'd just have to participate in the proposal process and present with all the other agencies that were "out there."

When you're an entrepreneur, and you look out of your office and see forty-plus employees, it can feel like a tremendous weight to bear. I knew that the team at the client did like us, but that they were confused about their own goals, waffling back and forth constantly. I also knew that because they were such a large client, we spent an inordinate amount of time servicing them, and their own lack of clarity created a lot of double work for us. They were one of our least profitable clients, but they were also one of our name brand clients—one that was sexy to future employees, clients, and acquirers. Also, might I remind you, they were 25 percent of our revenue.

So, what do you think I did? Did I pull up my big-girl pants, gather the team, and get crackin' on the RFP? Did I set out to do a big dog and pony show, showing off all of the great work we've done and setting a big grand vision of "coolness" for the future?

I absolutely did not.

I waited two days. I stared out at the staff, the weight of their payroll crushing me from the inside out. I calculated how much time we had left in our current contract, along with how much business I needed to generate to make up the revenue we'd be losing and start 2017 with a bang.

I sent an email directly to the CMO.

I wanted to let you know personally (and with great respect) that we are declining to participate in your RFP. As a business owner, I have a strong philosophy about RFPs. Even if I love the CMO (which I do) and I see the potential for the business (which I do), I don't believe that an incumbent agency should participate in an RFP for future business. The reality is that the decision to

RFP the business means that you feel that we are simply not "getting it." And, despite our success together, we have been unable to demonstrate to you that our strategic thinking will move your business forward. The resources, time, and effort we would spend trying to win your 2017 business is best spent ensuring that your end of year 2016 business is executed flawlessly—and our team will be engaged, excited, and pushing forward to get you great results.

This was one of my biggest "NO"s to date. It was damn scary to turn away from that RFP. But participating would be a waste of time and resources—kind of like trying desperately to win back a boyfriend who just isn't into you. I walked away with my head held high.

And yes, we replaced the revenue. Not without a lot of blood, sweat, and tears . . . but we did. With better business to boot.

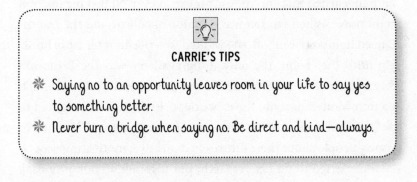

CARRIE'S TIPS

❋ Saying no to an opportunity leaves room in your life to say yes to something better.

❋ Never burn a bridge when saying no. Be direct and kind—always.

Learn to Love Saying "No" When You Need To

It's not only about learning to just *say* no. It's sometimes about learning to *love* no. Meet Lauren Berger, entrepreneur, author, and infamous Intern Queen.

While completing a staggering fifteen internships in college, Lauren learned a lot about who she was and who she wanted to be. After graduation, she moved out to Los Angeles, where she landed at Creative Artists Agency working as an assistant in the motion graphic talent department. All the while, she couldn't shake the idea that her internships had sparked: What if she was the face and voice behind career advice for young people? She knew from her own experiences that it was challenging to find internships, especially those in the business, public relations, and marketing spaces. Now, she wanted to *be* the place young people went to connect with their dream career opportunities. So with just $5,000 in the bank, Lauren launched InternQueen.com in 2009. She had no idea that the next few years would be full of "no." Learning to love rejection is one of the things that made Lauren's business so successful.

How did learning to love the word "no" help Lauren as a leader? Lauren learned that "no" doesn't mean "never." It just means "not right now." When Lauren was a senior in college and the Intern-Queen lightbulb went off, she wanted to write an internship book. Up until that point, the only thing available was the Princeton Review's *Internship Bible*, which was more like a giant textbook. Lauren wanted to write the exact opposite of that. She wanted to be "the Rachael Ray of the career and internship space," talking to young people about their futures in a positive, motivating way.

She started to do her research, put together a book proposal, sent it off to publishers and agents—and that's when the rejection letters poured in: "Lauren, internships are a topic that no one cares about. No one will publish this book. You have no platform, no credibility. It's never going to work."

But instead of giving in, Lauren took this harsh criticism constructively and decided to build a platform. Two years after launching InternQueen, she went back to the book and tried again, this time finding the right agent who made her literary dream a reality. The book was called *All Work, No Pay: Finding an Internship, Building Your Resume, Making Connections, and Gaining Job Experience*, and it became a national bestseller.

Lauren's brand grew to celebrity status. She became the voice for interns across America. But Lauren's perceived success does not mean that she rests on her laurels, or that she's constantly hearing "yes" from brands that she's pitching.

"People say, 'Oh, you must get so many phone calls,'" Lauren says with a laugh. "But I say, 'Oh no, I call everyone.'" Most of the time, people will say no at first, so Lauren follows up multiple times until she gets a yes. As she says, each no is one step closer to getting a yes. Either you get a "not now," which means that you can try to earn trust over time and get to yes, or you get a final "no," which means you move on to the next person who is likely a yes.

Lauren's advice for aspiring entrepreneurs, authors, and interns: Push yourself outside of your comfort zone. Don't take no for an answer. Write your own story. And FIO—figure it out.

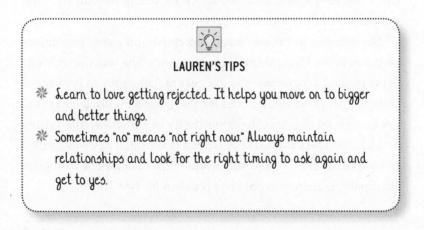

LAUREN'S TIPS

✳ Learn to love getting rejected. It helps you move on to bigger and better things.

✳ Sometimes "no" means "not right now." Always maintain relationships and look for the right timing to ask again and get to yes.

When No One Understands Why You'd Say No

One of my favorite FAB PAB members who sits at my table is Bev Thorne, who is currently the CMO of Freedom Mortgage. Bev has helped me throughout most of my time as CEO of Likeable; we connected when she was the CMO of Century 21 and I was charged with training her on her own personal social media usage. Immediately, I was fascinated by Bev—she was high energy, no nonsense, and just so incredibly smart. I started to devour every word she said—writing down her pearls of wisdom every chance I got. The truth is, Bev probably has a story for every single section of this book. But this story in particular caught me off guard, because when I think of someone who would never, ever be afraid of saying no, it would be Bev Thorne. This story that she shared with me about her early days in her career taught me that "becoming a Bev" takes time and practice.

The fourth of five siblings, Bev paid the majority of her own way through college. Following graduation, she knew that the only option for her was to get a job right out of school. She graduated on a Thursday, and her first job started on Monday. Of course, that's not so unusual for a hardworking young woman like Bev, but the job itself was quite impressive.

Bev was one of twelve recruits accepted into a very prestigious program at the Central Intelligence Agency. She was the only one of the twelve participants who did not graduate from an Ivy League college. This program, tailored for the group's eventual entry into the foreign service, was the opportunity of a lifetime. The vetting and selection process had taken over a year's time. Bev was thrilled to have been selected, and she accepted the assignment with great anticipation. There was only one problem for Bev Thorne.

Just days after she began the program, Bev discovered that she didn't like the very notion of the espionage work she was being asked to do at the CIA. In fact, she hated everything about it.

She hated the levels of security clearance she had to go through each day. She hated the material she had to learn and study. She hated that she would have to change her name and make up a fake occupation. While all of her program peers were relishing every moment of the opportunity, Bev was left feeling utterly conflicted.

First of all, after having paid her way through college, she was not used to the notion of money coming to her—she was used to paying it out. She wasn't aware it was even possible to tell someone who paid you that, thanks, but no thanks, you're not interested in this highly coveted position. Second, she couldn't imagine telling her friends and family that she was leaving a job she just started, let alone a job that was so impressive to the outside world.

For several months she struggled with the realization that the reality of the job was very different from what her vision of it had been. On paper, the job was a perfect fit—she had planned to go to law school, and this was the absolute perfect career step for her. Unfortunately, every day that she stayed at the CIA it became clearer that it was not a good fit. She recalls, "One morning I got a flat tire on the way to work. You would have thought that I was a decorated dignitary stranded on the side of the road, because several policemen and the Secret Service came to my aid, sent to find me when it was reported in Langley that I was fifteen minutes late for work. They sent out a search team. For them, it was standard practice—they seemed convinced that I hadn't reported to work because I was attacked by someone who wanted proprietary foreign intelligence information that I had. Later that day, my friends buzzed about how cool it was. I didn't think it was cool at all."

Early that fall, Bev finally found the courage to tell the CIA officials that she was not interested in continuing on the path to the Foreign Service Corps. After reinitiating conversations with companies that had recruited her on campus during college, she accepted a job with the Chesapeake & Potomac Telephone Company (which later became AT&T). Here's the funny part of the story—the position she accepted was an "account executive." When she arrived at training on her first day, she was surprised. "I said, excuse me, sir? This is a sales training. I accepted an account executive job." Bev was too young and too inexperienced to know that an account executive job was in fact a sales job.

Very early on, she was again conflicted. She thought all sales jobs were equivalent to a used car salesperson job, and she didn't like the vision. What was she going to tell her parents? From CIA agent to telephone sales? This was unheard of. Turns out, the opposite of what happened at the CIA happened here. Her vision had again been wrong—but this time, reality was far better than her vision.

Just days after she began, Bev was in love with the job. She loved sales, so much so that she started outselling her peers who had been there for many years. Her early sales success led to multiple promotions, and eventually, to receiving an incredible honor: AT&T sponsored her to earn her MBA at Wharton, one of the most prestigious business schools in the country. She stayed at C&P Telephone as they merged with and ultimately became the behemoth that is AT&T, rising in the ranks of corporate America. Needless to say, she made her parents, and herself, very proud. All from learning to say no when something that seemed so great to others just didn't feel right to her.

BEV'S TIPS

✳ Sometimes, something can be totally right on paper. But if it doesn't feel right, it's probably not.

✳ The pressure to continue on a path that family and friends are "proud of" can be really hard. But picture how proud YOU'LL be when you're doing what truly feels right to you.

EXERCISE THREE

The "Carrie Method" for Effective Decision-Making

If there's one thing I learned from the women of this book, it's that

using your gut is key to succeeding in life. But a lot of times I had trouble figuring out what my gut wanted, and whether it was aligned with the facts in front of me. I created the "Carrie Method" to help myself—and now you—make effective decisions based on a crucial combination of instinct and intellect.

Current Situation	Available Options	Repercussions	Rewards	Intuition	End Result
Use the space below to write a description of the current situation. Be brief—no more than two sentences—which will force you to take a bird's-eye view.	Use the space below to list every available option to you—no matter how silly. List them in bulleted form.	In the space below, list a potential risk or repercussion associated with each of the available options you listed in the box to the left. Write them in the same order as the options to keep your answers consistent and easy to compare across the columns.	For each available option, list the potential rewards below. (Remember, these rewards can be more than monetary.)	For each of these options—try the stomachache test. Close your eyes and try to envision yourself making the decision. How do you feel? Sometimes, with a hard decision, none of the options feel great. But one will feel better than the others. In the box below, rate on a scale of 1–10 (1 being not right at all and 10 being completely right) how much the available option just "feels right."	Theodore Roosevelt said, "In any moment of decision, the best thing you can do is the right thing, the next best thing is the wrong thing, and the worst thing you can do is nothing." The ladies of WORK IT concur. Write your decision down below. Read it out loud and step away from it. Come back, and read it out loud again. How do you feel?

CHAPTER 9

Engage Your Inner Entre-, Intra-, or Nontrepreneur

Sometimes, ideas come to me in phrases. I don't think I'd have thought of the podcast, for instance, without thinking of the name *All the Social Ladies*. When I was preparing to give a speech to entrepreneurs at Baruch College, the only thing that kept going through my head was, "I'm not an entrepreneur, I'm a nontrepreneur."

I wasn't surprised that I felt like that. The start of our business certainly wasn't planned. When my husband wanted to fulfill his dream of having a massively large wedding, we brainstormed and planned a home run of an affair—quite literally. We were married in front of five thousand people at the Brooklyn Cyclones stadium at the conclusion of a baseball game. The wedding and game were sponsored by wedding vendors—all of whom got a ton of press for participating. When sponsors like 1-800-Flowers.com came to us asking us to "do it again," we started a word-of-mouth marketing company. We didn't plan to start a company, let alone one that would take off like this. It just kind of happened.

Normally, when I recount this story, I sound like a badass entrepreneur. An entrepreneur is bold, brave, confident, and loves taking risks. An entrepreneur knows which way the wind blows before there's even a slight breeze. An entrepreneur has it all together. And being an entrepreneur with "the only company founded on her wedding day" sounds like a fairy tale.

The reality is, it wasn't quite so dreamy.

I didn't actually leave my job to start the company right after the wedding. In fact, I was afraid to pull the trigger. That is, until a trigger pulled me.

I had a three-year-old daughter named Charlotte from a previous marriage whom I was raising on my own. When you're a parent, the need for stability and security can outweigh the desire to pursue your own business—and even though I knew the wedding was a hit, I didn't want to risk starting my own thing and failing my daughter. I continued at my sales manager position, which was an hour's commute from home.

One morning, Charlotte simply didn't want me to leave her side. As I was dropping her off at day care, she grabbed my leg, looked up at me with her wide, almond-shaped eyes, and said, "Mommy. Don't go."

I didn't.

The truth is, I wasn't thinking about building a multimillion-dollar business. I was thinking about one thing and one thing only:

The freedom to spend time with Charlotte.

I took the day off, and planned out my income potential. I knew that Dave's job would give us benefits and a good starting base salary—and I knew I wouldn't make anywhere near as much as I did as a sales manager—but I plotted out what I needed to make and worked backward from there. What sponsor could I call? What event could I plan? How could I hit my income goals?

There was no business plan. There was nothing other than a desire to earn the bare minimum needed to pay for my complete and total freedom. And I knew that I could get there.

The next day, I gave my notice.

I thought back to this story as I began to plan my speech for Baruch College. Entrepreneurs take risks at all costs. Nontrepreneurs take calculated risks. Entrepreneurs have sizzle—they have an underlying confidence that seems unending. Nontrepreneurs are the ones who are riding the entrepreneurial roller coaster with their hands over their eyes, clutching their purses and praying they don't fall off. Entrepreneurs know what to do. Nontrepreneurs ask others what to do.

I wrote my speech and delivered it to a crowd of entrepreneurs and received a standing ovation. Turns out, even the most badass of entrepreneurs feel like nontrepreneurs sometimes.

🔆

CARRIE'S TIPS

❋ The risks you take should be calculated. If you're leaving your job to start a business, plot out your earning potential and plan for rainy days as well.

❋ Just because you're an entrepreneur doesn't mean you have to feel or act like a "badass" 100 percent of the time.

Start as Soon as You Can

Because I had a three-year-old when starting our business, there was a lot of risk in my taking the leap. For entrepreneurs who start early, the sky can be the limit. Just ask Victoria Ransom, the tech entrepreneur who sold her company for $450 million to Google.

When I think of the most successful tech entrepreneurs, picking asparagus doesn't usually come to mind. Unless I'm thinking about my dear friend Victoria Ransom, the daughter of an asparagus farmer from Scott's Ferry, New Zealand, home to just sixty-five people. That's where she grew up and where, as a child, she first displayed her love of entrepreneurship, picking asparagus and selling it to the fishermen who fished nearby. Victoria moved to America and attended college, starting as a Wall Street analyst right after graduation. "I knew I wasn't going to love it, but I figured I would try something that could open as many doors as possible for me."

Victoria and her then-boyfriend Alain visited an entrepreneur friend in Canada, who ran ski and snowboard camps for kids. Victoria was intrigued; he loved his job fully, and was living what seemed like a dream life. Victoria and Alain brainstormed on what type of business they could start based on their own passions. They decided to build an entire company based on passion—starting a travel company that allowed people to plan trips based on hobbies they loved, like surfing and snowboarding. In 2001, they both quit their high-powered banking jobs, moved to New Zealand, and started Access Trips. At this point in their lives, with no kids, and almost fresh out of college, their primary thought around entrepreneurship was, "What do we have to lose? The worst thing that happens is it fails and we have to get jobs in corporate again. It didn't feel like such a risk to us at that point in our lives."

As Access Trips grew, Victoria wanted to experiment with online marketing for the company. They wanted to give away a free trip on Facebook, but, at the time, you couldn't post a promotion like that on Facebook; you needed to use a third-party application. There was no software anywhere that met this need. They decided to build it. In 2008, their second company, Wildfire, was born, an app that allowed users to design promotions on Facebook, without having to pay for a developer. Since options for this kind of software were very limited at the time, clients started to pour in. Suddenly, Victoria found herself running a software company. She and Alain sold Access Trips and got to work.

When you hear the stories of these tech juggernauts at the time, they seem like fairy tales. *Oh, we were operating at a $100 million loss and we raised a billion dollars*—these types of tales were heard all throughout the Valley. Not so for Victoria and Alain. They found that due to the business climate in 2008, venture capitalists were skittish. Recognizing this, Victoria and Alain decided to bootstrap the entire operation. They worked out of their living room, hiring developers in Estonia, and salespeople based on commission. Unlike just about every other tech startup in 2008, Victoria and Alain were profitable within year one of operating the business—again, having less to lose than if they raised massive funds and disappointed investors.

If the first step was becoming profitable, the second step was becoming an integral partner to the platform on which their business depended: Facebook. Alain and Victoria called on every friend they had at Facebook . . . pitching everyone they knew about how Wildfire could help Facebook achieve their goals of getting brands to invest heavily in the network. The plan worked, and the duo were not only awarded a $250,000 grant from the fbFund, but they became known throughout the organization.

It was the relationship with Facebook that caught the attention of Google. Google had a series of failed attempts at social media efforts—Google Wave and Google+, for example. When they saw Wildfire and their close insight into the Facebook operation, they wanted in. They bought Wildfire for $450 million.

Suddenly, Victoria went from being an entrepreneur to being an employee of Google—which was disorienting, but not necessarily for the reasons you'd think. "I hear so many stories of founders that became so micromanaged. At Google, the philosophy is to let you figure it out. So we were plopped into their infrastructure, and we felt a bit lost initially. We had to figure out how to meet Google's goals instead of our own—but with limited guidance."

As soon as they were able to, Victoria and Alain left Google to start their most meaningful project of all: their family. "I cannot imagine how difficult it would have been to build something like Wildfire and have a family," Victoria said. "I made a conscious decision to wait, and for me, that worked."

Victoria and Alain are spending some time hanging with their two children, Elle and Nicolas, and are quietly working on their next venture. Once an entrepreneur, always an entrepreneur.

VICTORIA'S TIPS

❋ If you know you want to be an entrepreneur, start early. When you're young and you start a business, there's much less risk.

❋ Bootstrap as much as you possibly can to get to where you want to be.

Don't Worry about Being a Trendsetter—Be a Trendspotter

Some people start their entrepreneurial journey way before Victoria did. Still, when someone talks about running a business over the span of twenty years, you don't really assume that they're in their mid-thirties. For Tina Wells, the CEO and founder of millennial marketing agency Buzz Marketing Group, work began at fifteen years old.

At fifteen, Tina saw an ad in the back of *Seventeen* magazine, seeking writers for a girls' newspaper called the *New Girls Times*. She was hired as a product review writer and she would receive product in exchange for a review. Tina took great pride in her reviews, and she'd clip them out and mail a copy to each company whose product she had reviewed. The companies were so thrilled with her work, they'd ask if they could send her more things to look at and review.

A self-described "product junkie," Tina leaped at the opportunity to review more and more of her favorite things. After all, as the eldest of six kids, you didn't exactly get every product you wanted all the time.

While still in high school, Tina continued to trade reviews for products and she started expanding her reach. Tina recalls when PR powerhouse agency LaForce & Stevens invited her to New York at age eighteen for a meeting—except they had no idea that she was just a kid. They were the ones to first call Tina a "trendspotter"—a term that resonated with her—giving a name to this mythical accidental career she had started. But there were a whole lot of products in the world, and there was only one Tina.

Tina earned a lot of cool cred with her friends. She'd start giving product to her friends to help. Those friends recruited other friends. Tina's trendspotting movement started to spread. Of course, in those days, if you were lucky, you had just gotten an AOL email address, so it wasn't as easy to grow—but the teen-to-teen network started expanding as rapidly as it could in a pre-digital era. Suddenly, Tina had twenty-five "employees," receiving product in exchange for reviews.

After graduating from high school, Tina kept the business going, and in college she decided to work with a professor to develop a business plan.

"I remember the moment my professor told me I would be an entrepreneur. I would stay up all night crafting a document. The professor would rip it apart. I'd take the feedback, albeit brutal, I'd go back, and do it again. That's when she said she knew." She spent thirteen weeks refining her business plans, and Buzz Marketing Group was born.

Through a connection, Tina was asked if she'd like to be featured in *CosmoGirl*'s new section highlighting cool, young female entrepreneurs. She gladly accepted, and asked that they put a line in that helped her recruit more trendspotters. They actually included two sentences. They read:

"Cool Job Alert! Be a Trendspotter!"

Suddenly, Tina had fifteen thousand applications from people all over the world.

They had just built their first Web site, and suddenly, it crashed. This was the big moment for Buzz Marketing Group, and Tina was not throwing away her shot. She hired nine thousand people, forming a broad network of thirteen- to nineteen-year-olds who did exactly what she once did—sampling. But now, instead of writing reviews for Tina, they were giving her critical insight to form trend research.

As time went on, Tina used her keen abilities as a trendspotter to find trends that would benefit her own business. The trend that catapulted her forward the fastest? The dawn of the millennial generation. All of those teenagers she'd been covering in the late '90s? They grew up and became millennials. And millennials were all anyone was talking about. Tina decided to own her position as a millennial marketer—providing research on what is now considered the most influential generation in recent history.

Tina's success is much less about her own need to stand out and be a trendsetter, and much more about reflecting the trends that are happening around her—and capitalizing on them to meet the needs of a rapidly changing marketplace.

TINA'S TIPS

❋ Don't just look at the trends happening today—look at the effects those trends will have, and what that will mean for the future. Always be thinking two steps ahead when planning your business.

❋ As an entrepreneur, you have to be comfortable getting knocked down over and over again.

Don't Get Attached to Everything You Build

Tina started at sixteen years old, which begs the question, are we born with entrepreneurial qualities, or are they bred? How does one know that they have what it takes to be an entrepreneur? Caroline Ghosn, founder and CEO of Levo, was displaying entrepreneurial qualities from the minute she was born.

Caroline cofounded Levo, a professional network dedicated to helping millennials navigate the workplace. They've raised over $9 million of angel investment and are considered one of the go-to destinations for millennials in the workplace. I asked Caroline what single quality made her best able to handle the ups and downs of entrepreneurship. Her answer was simple: the ability to be detached. And that was learned from a very young age.

As early as age five, she remembers sitting in her garage with her mother, working a potter's wheel. "We would build piece after piece. I'd hate some of them. Some of them would fall over. I learned very early on not to get attached to every single thing you build. They don't all work out."

That critical lesson of learning to accept and move on from failure carried throughout her life. "I was obsessed, and I mean *obsessed*, with the video game called *The Sims*. I'd build an entire world in *The Sims*—this virtual reality. It would be so elaborate, so detailed—and just like that, I'd die and have to start over. Gamers have similar qualities to entrepreneurs. You build something, you die. Over and over again. Gamers don't really give a fuck when they die. They might be pissed for a minute, but they just start again."

After attending Stanford, Caroline joined McKinsey & Company to learn the ins and outs of business. She soon discovered that she wasn't cut out for the corporate world. Yet, although she displayed so many entrepreneurial qualities, she felt afraid to take the leap. Again, she connects this time to a memory from childhood and to an essential quality necessary for entrepreneurship: a willingness to be pushed, by yourself, or by those around you.

"I remember when I was little and learning to swim, I would stand outside of the pool, analyzing it, terrified to get in. My mom wanted to throw me in and just let me figure it out—my dad was totally against it. Turns out, she did, and boy, did I love it. I just needed that little push. Now, I swim the Alcatraz Sharkfest Swim, but I wonder what would have happened if I didn't have that little push back when I was a kid."

It turns out, in order to leave McKinsey and start the company of her dreams, she needed another little push, this time from fellow McKinsey employee and eventual Levo cofounder, Amanda Pouchot. "She was the one who encouraged me to really 'preneur myself. And once I did, I never looked back."

The result? Levo's vibrant community now engages over ten million young professionals with thirty chapters around the world where fifty thousand members meet up in person to connect and learn.

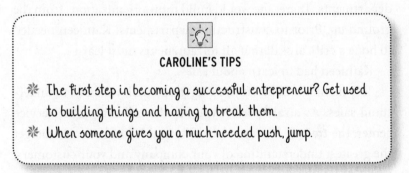

CAROLINE'S TIPS

❋ The first step in becoming a successful entrepreneur? Get used to building things and having to break them.

❋ When someone gives you a much-needed push, jump.

Be an Intrapreneur (An Entrepreneur in the Corporate World)

Being an entrepreneur means taking a big risk. Having the qualities of an entrepreneur while working in a big organization, however? That's a lower-risk recipe for success. Just ask Kathleen Curtis Wolf, who I met when she was a senior manager of corporate reputation and interactive communications at Whirlpool Corporation.

Kathleen is from a family of small business owners. Watching her brothers and sisters work long hours every weekend convinced her that being an entrepreneur wasn't for her. She decided to take a path that let her use her creative entrepreneurial skills within the balanced confines of corporate America.

Kathleen became an intrapreneur.

An intrapreneur looks for roles within organizations where they can go in, understand and learn about an emerging space, and figure out what they can do to bring it to the next level. In seeking out these roles, Kathleen uses the entrepreneurial quality that resonates with her most—the ability to build things from scratch.

While at Whirlpool Corporation, Kathleen raised her hand for new opportunities—particularly when it came to forming new departments. There, she would build mini-organizations from the ground up. Prior to constructing departments, Kathleen needed to hone a critical skill that all intrapreneurs must learn.

Kathleen had to learn about sales.

"My mentor told me, if you want to do well, you need to understand sales. As a salesperson you are the call center, the service center, the trainer . . . you're all of it. In this kind of role, you get the greatest understanding of your company and your customers, and it's a lot like running your own business."

When her mentor was tapped to start the first e-business unit within the company, Kathleen had the sales experience, and was trained and ready to build something entirely new. Kathleen began as one of the first female salespeople selling construction projects at Whirlpool Corporation through the Internet. This was entirely uncharted territory for Whirlpool Corporation.

It's not surprising that Kathleen was one of the very first to start developing systems and processes for social media at Whirlpool

Corporation shortly after building out the e-business. In social media, the networks change constantly—providing Kathleen with a chance to rebuild social strategies from within the organization, time and time again. That's the sign of a true intrapreneur.

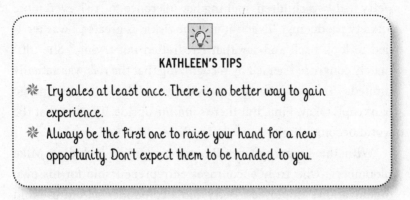

KATHLEEN'S TIPS

※ Try sales at least once. There is no better way to gain experience.

※ Always be the first one to raise your hand for a new opportunity. Don't expect them to be handed to you.

Start a Side Hustle

There's intrapreneurship, and then there's the concept that has now been artfully described as the "side hustle": when you build your business while keeping your full-time job. The art of the side hustle is well documented, and the opinions are truly divided. Some think it's not truly committing to your business, while others think it's a smart way to decrease your risk potential.

One big fan of the side hustle is Betty Liu, currently both an anchor on Bloomberg Television and the CEO and founder of Radiate, a media technology platform that features business advice from top leaders in the business world.

Betty always remembers having a bit of an entrepreneurial bug, but was also pretty risk averse. Graduating from college right before the dot-com bubble burst, Betty saw many of her friends building businesses and losing them, all within a few years' time.

She suppressed her entrepreneurial tendencies and went on with her career, becoming a successful television anchor.

Betty couldn't shake the feeling that she wanted more, but the situation now was a bit different: no longer fresh out of college, Betty had two children, making her tolerance for risk even more anxiety producing. "Even though the risk was greater, I was terrified to look back and say that I regretted not trying." She ultimately convinced herself by recognizing that the risk was actually limited. "There is a finite downside: your idea fails and you go bankrupt. Okay. Fine. But there's *infinite* upside. The fact that the world becomes limitless is what really excited me."

With the support of her Bloomberg family, including Mike Bloomberg, who truly encourages entrepreneurship for his own organization's employees, Betty and a cofounder set out to build Radiate. Betty kept her full-time position, and she's not sure if it held her back. "I know it's allowed me to be more methodical, and I know I'm happy with my own pace. I won't ever know what it would have been like if I was doing this full-time, I might have gone faster."

Perhaps speed would have been a disadvantage for Betty. Working at Bloomberg, she's interviewed countless entrepreneurs. She's heard all the fairy tales and all of the stories—"Oh, this one had a high burn rate, this one had a huge office, this one has a huge team." Betty believes that this is why many of these businesses fail. "The only thing that matters is doing what's right for you and your company. It was important for me not to get caught up in all of the advice that I now feel was exactly what I *shouldn't* do."

After Betty raised $1 million in seed funding, it was time to hold their first meeting and get started. She learned quickly that being an entrepreneur is about more than just taking a risk. It's about doing all kinds of new things. There were so many questions that she hadn't thought of. "I sat down for the first-ever company meeting and I was like—okay, now what do we do? Nobody tells you how to start your first meeting. And asking a question like that to someone? It's like the equivalent of asking someone, 'How do I eat?'"

Being an entrepreneur is just like anything else—you have to put one foot in front of the other and learn as you go.

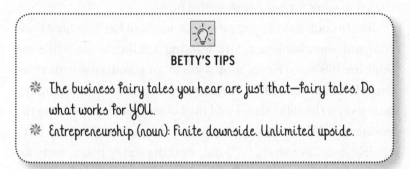

BETTY'S TIPS

✳ The business fairy tales you hear are just that—fairy tales. Do what works for YOU.
✳ Entrepreneurship (noun): Finite downside. Unlimited upside.

The Buck Stops with You

Betty's not the only entrepreneur I know who built her business in a more calculated way. This entrepreneur entirely self-funded her business and grew it into a business powerhouse without raising funds, or ever fully leaving her job.

The day after her twenty-fourth birthday, Kevin Gilbert left her home country of Venezuela for America. She spoke three languages, so finding a job was easy. She landed at an employment firm, where she managed the office. Unfortunately, the business itself was a mess. Her boss was a big spender—investing in technology that didn't help the recruiters at all. Kevin felt concerned that the business was going to go under—and she wanted the ability to truly understand the finances that her boss so poorly managed.

Kevin enrolled at NYU at night—to get her degree in accounting and finance, determined to start her own business on the side. "For me, I was just sick of blaming my boss. I was very big on ownership. I wanted the buck to stop with me." So when her boss was unable to manage the temp portion of his staffing business, Kevin formed her own small staffing company, all while she continued to work for her irresponsible boss.

It turns out, Kevin's gut was right-on about her boss, and their company went bankrupt. Still wanting a full-time job while she built her business, Kevin took a job at an accounting firm as an entry-level accountant. "I took a pay cut, but I was building my business on the side. Also, I told my bosses that I was building the business and they were fine with it so long as I worked my forty billable hours per week. So, I did, working eighty hours, forty for the firm and forty for my business."

Eventually, Kevin won a small contract at Chase Bank, and gradually grew it to the point where her company provided maintenance services to over a thousand branches in the Northeast. The contract built out her business, and she easily could have worked on it full-time. Instead, she simply reduced her hours with the accounting firm, maintaining key relationships with clients and enjoying the work.

Kevin also teaches classes for women entrepreneurs. The primary lesson she teaches is around ownership and accountability. The two words she'd like to erase from the dictionary? "*If only*. I hear it all the time—if only I hadn't lost that client. If only my husband would change. If only. The reality is, the buck stops with you. If I can teach young entrepreneurs that lesson, I can teach them to take ownership and responsibility for their lives, to live fully, with no resentments or regrets."

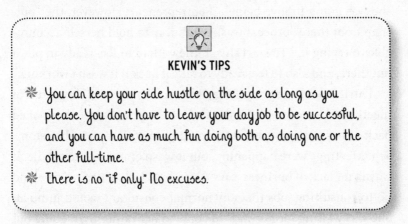

KEVIN'S TIPS

✳ You can keep your side hustle on the side as long as you please. You don't have to leave your day job to be successful, and you can have as much fun doing both as doing one or the other full-time.

✳ There is no "if only." No excuses.

You Don't Have to Be an Entrepreneur to Have a Bold and Brilliant Career

No matter how many entrepreneurial qualities you think you have, the only way to really know if you're cut out to be an entrepreneur is to try. It doesn't always work out. Aliza Licht had spent seventeen years at DKNY, and was in the role of SVP, global communications. She'd built their Twitter following to over half a million followers, transforming herself into a character called DKNY PR GIRL. She'd just released a book called *Leave Your Mark: Land Your Dream Job. Kill It in Your Career. Rock Social Media.* It was safe to say Aliza was at the top of her game. Now she was ready for her next move. Craving flexibility, new challenges, and the pursuit of creative passions, Aliza left her highly coveted "dream job" at DKNY in December 2015 to start a consulting company.

For Aliza, who comes from a PR background, everything about becoming an entrepreneur was about putting it out there.

She developed a name, a logo, a Web site, and launched loudly and publicly. The only problem? Aliza was not 100 percent sure that she was going to love being an entrepreneur. However, the "putting it out there" process was Aliza's way to hold herself accountable to trying it. "To start this, I knew I had to feel ready to put it out there, and also to feel ready to take it back if it wasn't working."

During her time consulting, Aliza's calendar was chock-full of meetings. However, when the end of the year came, she looked back at her first year of entrepreneurship with a pit in her stomach. Meetings were happening, but it wasn't moving the needle. It wasn't for lack of business, says Aliza, but "lack of desire." She said no to consulting jobs that any normal consultant would jump at. She was waiting for business to come to her rather than going out and getting it. So, at the end of this almost one-year stint, she had to ask herself the tough question: WHY?

It turns out that what Aliza had really wanted when she left her job was a break. She was wooed by the allure of "entrepreneurship." Really what she wanted and needed was time to energize her brain, freshen her mind-set, and reboot her passion.

After ten months of "entrepreneurship," Aliza joined the team of alice + olivia by Stacey Bendet as the EVP of brand marketing and communications. She put that out there, too, in true Aliza form, writing a post for *Forbes* that was shared far and wide, titled: "This Is How You Know You're Not Meant to Be an Entrepreneur."

Says Aliza, "I don't fear missing out on the startup life. I don't fear not being my own boss. My power lies in being honest enough with myself to know when the path has ended and I need to make a turn. It's about understanding my strengths and my weaknesses and learning how to apply the strengths to enhance my growth."

Sometimes, we need to try entrepreneurship to know it's not for us.

ALIZA'S TIPS

✽ Entrepreneurship is very "hot" right now—but it's not for everyone, and that's okay.

✽ When you're doing something that doesn't make you feel good, ask yourself the hardest question: WHY?

CHAPTER 10

Fail Fantastically

WHETHER YOU'RE AN entrepreneur, an intrapreneur, a nontrepreneur, or an employee—one thing is certain—you will fail. One of my biggest regrets in life was not playing sports as a kid. I never really learned how to lose. And what I found was that as I got older, I simply avoided things I wasn't good at. This helped me to avoid failure, but it also kept me from learning. Over time, I started failing—and I learned that the more I did, and the more I embraced it, the better my successes actually became. Here's a story of one of my first failures as the CEO of Likeable.

When I stepped into the CEO role at Likeable, I inherited the new clients that were sold into the company the year prior. This included a government agency located in the Middle East, for which we were hired to create a global social media playbook—basically, giving them the tools to execute social across their hundreds of different departments and programs within the agency. This was a lofty goal for any client, but for a client that was headquartered overseas when we were not yet a global agency it seemed almost impossible. I let the team continue the work on the project, and I wasn't surprised when I got a call from the head of the aforementioned agency.

"Carrie," she said. "I am very unhappy with your company's work, and this is not what Dave promised me. I'd like to meet with you personally."

I agreed to meet, filled with my usual rush of "I can fix this" energy. I sat in a room with them at their New York office. I asked them to start from the beginning—to tell me what they wanted, and I'd do my best to help solve.

The organization was complex: they had multiple goals, and the people in the room weren't aligned on which to pursue or how to execute them. My superwoman complex took over, and I put my neck on the line.

I said, "The only way I can really understand the complex infrastructure of this organization is to go to your headquarters overseas to interview the key stakeholders and learn about the ins and outs of the organization. I will spend a week with your team, deliver you a global playbook, and if you're not happy at that point, I will refund the money you've paid us."

What was I thinking? I'd take a week away from my family, travel overseas, do a ton of work, and refund their money based on a subjective evaluation of my work? Nuts. In my mind, they'd never ask for their money back after I did all that work. And besides, I was the best in the business.

They were thrilled with the idea. My best team member and I headed off to a foreign land to learn the ins and outs of their government agency and their five hundred–plus programs to benefit their country. For a full week, we were in an office building, hosting meetings upon meetings. I had a great idea of what they needed to do. The team seemed thrilled, and my plan had worked. I flew home feeling quite proud of myself.

When the time came to present the playbook, the team was repeatedly unavailable to meet. I chalked it up to time zones, or to tight schedules . . . and I just kept pressing them. Two months later, they agreed to hear the playbook results, over the phone, with no screen sharing. All two hundred pages, delivered over the phone, in one hour.

I delivered the playbook presentation—the document that took me out of the office for one week and out of my company's leadership focus for three weeks—with heart. At the end, they said two words: "Thank you." They hung up the phone.

The next day, I received a letter from their agency's lawyer. "As per our agreement, you will refund our money. We are not happy with your product. Thank you."

My own ego had caused me to make a brutal mistake on behalf of the company. A six-figure, weeks-of-wasted-time, morale-busting failure.

After consulting with our own attorneys, I decided that returning the money was better than the potential legal fees and smearing of our name, which was what this agency threatened to do should we move forward. I set a plan for how we'd build our cash back up and just moved forward.

CARRIE'S TIPS

❋ Red Flag Alert: When you come across a problem that "only you" can solve, that's your ego talking. Take a step back and find another solution.

❋ The sooner you can admit failure and walk away, the sooner you can focus on your next success.

Embrace Failure, Rather Than Avoiding It

It's quite an amazing thing when you're friends with someone, and you watch them catapult into superstardom. For my friend Reshma Saujani, that trip to entrepreneur superstardom didn't come without a few hiccups along the way.

In 2016, Reshma, then founder of the nonprofit Girls Who Code, gave a speech titled "Teach Girls Bravery, Not Perfection." To date, it has over three million views. In it, she tells the story of her first run for Congress—a race she was pegged to win. Instead, she received just 19 percent of the votes, roughly six thousand voters. She spent $1.3 million on the campaign. It was an epic failure by any account. Reshma tells us in her speech that we need to stop raising our girls to be perfect and avoid failure at all costs. Instead, we need to teach our girls to be brave.

Reshma's speech was primarily focused on the future—on today's girls who would be tomorrow's leaders and what we need to do for them. I remember watching her and thinking, *Gosh, Reshma failed and bounced back, and now she wants others to feel okay doing the same. I need to get comfortable failing, too.* But, as Reshma reminds us, we are conditioned from an early age to avoid failure. I needed to get over that. So I called my dear friend, and asked her some follow-up questions about what happens after you fail.

For Reshma, it was all about setting a finite time to grieve. The day after her loss in her Congressional run was awful. She had zero intention of losing—wouldn't even let the thought enter her mind. So, when she did, she wasn't ready to just pick up and move forward. She needed to grieve. "I picked a finite amount of time to grieve. And then, I moved forward." Reshma lost in September— and it took her until December to be able to take a meeting again. She was okay with that, of course, because she allowed herself that time.

Because "you can't run a campaign thinking about a backup plan," Reshma had no idea what she wanted to do next. So when December came around, she took lots of meetings, and figured out what was next by process of elimination. She knew that she didn't want to work in the private sector again. She knew that eventually she wanted to run again, but maybe not today. She knew that, above all, she wanted to do some good. That's when she founded Girls Who Code, a national nonprofit organization dedicated to closing the gender gap in technology, which has since taught over forty thousand girls coding skills.

RESHMA'S TIPS

❋ After a failure, allow yourself a fixed amount of time to wallow. When that time is up, #workit.

❋ Practicing the art of failure builds bravery and ultimately success. Think about how you can eliminate the need for perfection from your life today, and take steps to do so.

Build Up a Credibility Bank

Many years ago, before Candie Harris was my client, my friend, or my business partner, she was a product manager at Esselte, an office supply manufacturing and marketing company. She was in charge of the launch of a new product line that would replace an older one. Esselte had inventory of the old product, and the transition to the supply of the new product would be complicated. Candie's job was to manage that transition—watching the inventory like a hawk.

Candie swore she was on top of the transition, but she was unable to get rid of the old supply before bringing the new product in. This cost Esselte a lot of money, and cost Candie a ton of credibility.

Candie was devastated. "I felt like I had personally let down the president of the company, and I couldn't believe I thought I had this under control when I didn't." From that day forward, Candie vowed to focus on the details—especially around anything that affects finances. Certain that she'd be fired, Candie immediately went to her boss and took accountability for the error. It turns out, although her credibility was damaged, Esselte continued to invest in Candie. This is where Candie first discovered the concept of the "credibility bank."

"Every person has what I call a credibility bank. When you start a new job or a new position, you have zero in your credibility bank because you have no relationship and you haven't yet done anything. As you perform, you gain 'dollars' or credibility in your bank so that if you do mess up or you do need to ask for a special favor out of the ordinary, it's no problem because you've built up this bank. You can deplete on your bank when you mess up, but you can build it back up and then some."

When Candie made her error, her credibility bank was pretty full. She'd done a lot of great work. When the error happened, her credibility was damaged but nowhere near done. She focused on building her credibility back up. Candie's strategy worked—staying with Esselte for over twenty-five years, ultimately becoming a global vice president.

CANDIE'S TIPS

❊ Everyone has a credibility bank. How can you build yours? Take steps on a regular basis to work on building it, as you never know when it will save you during a crisis or failure.

❊ When you screw up, take accountability for it immediately.

Know When to Hold 'em and When to Fold 'em

There's no failure that hurts quite like that of an entrepreneur whose business doesn't make it. As someone who grew up most of her life with the name "Carrie Fisher," I had a special appreciation for my dear friend Bea Arthur. When you share a name with a famous celebrity, it's an instant conversation starter. With Bea, it wouldn't be hard to start a conversation anyway—she's the kind of person that you just want to talk to. It's no surprise that she pursued a career as a therapist.

During her time as a therapist, she kept thinking to herself, *It should be easier to do this. People should be able to talk when they need it, where they need it.* An idea was born. Bea started Pretty Padded Room, a Web site portal offering convenient, low-cost therapy online for women. She ran it for three years, and the press loved it. Bea was receiving a lot of attention.

Bea really just wanted to run a therapy company, but because she'd put this online, she was running a tech company, too. Things would break constantly, and Bea felt totally out of her element. It didn't help that the New York investor community she'd approached to get funding to hire employees, refused to take her seriously. Her gut was saying to close up shop— until Jessica Livingston, the founder of Y Combinator, known as the "world's most powerful startup incubator," saw something in Bea and in Pretty Padded Room. She encouraged Bea to apply for funding through Y Combinator. Whereas the NY tech scene didn't take Bea seriously, Y Combinator believed in her, and she was the first African American woman to apply and receive funds. Between Y Combinator and friends and family, Bea raised $600,000. Bea was growing the business very quickly at the same time, from $14,000 to $42,000 per month in billings. Since most startups that received funding in the Valley were not even making any revenue yet, Bea was feeling good.

Newly funded, Bea decided that she should rebrand, believing that men needed online therapy even more than women did, particularly because they were more reluctant to seek treatment when struggling. She renamed the company In Your Corner. Unfortunately, the rebrand cost her a massive amount of time and money. During the four months she was in "stealth planning mode," a lot happened in the industry. A few competitors popped up and they were raising tens of millions of dollars rather quickly. Bea's gut started nagging at her again that something didn't feel right. But every time she even entertained the slightest notion of closing up shop, something great would happen. She'd get coverage in Buzz-Feed, or she'd find an amazing new advisor. "I just couldn't picture closing. It seemed totally unfathomable."

The business never fully recovered, and in 2015, she had to lay people off. Not only that, but she had borrowed money from "predatory" high-interest lenders that drove her monthly payments to over $9,000 per month. She was working nonstop and exhausted. "I felt like the janitor instead of the CEO," says Bea. It was time to ask advisors for help.

Bea texted her advisor, famed investor and entrepreneur Gina Bianchini. Her response?

"Call me. Now."

Gina, famous for pulling no punches, told her to close up shop. "You've got a cute name. You're great on camera. As an entrepreneur, though, no one's going to take you seriously. You should be in front of a TV screen, not stuck behind a computer screen."

Bea remembers feeling overwhelmed with relief. This was a lightbulb moment for her, and she started making plans to close. And then, she took a wrong turn.

Bea was at home in her pajamas, working on her year-end finances, when she saw that she made over $400,000 in revenue in the last year, despite all of her hardships. "Why am I wasting time trying to get money from investors when I should've been focused on getting money the old-fashioned way: from happy customers." Bea was reenergized and determined to make the company work once and for all, but looking back, she describes it as "a moment of false hope and resurgence." She had gotten her second wind, but she was missing the writing on the wall.

A few months after deciding not to close, two therapists who worked for Bea stole all of her data and started a competitor company. Bea was in the same place—the pipe dream of suddenly raising enough money from customers to make the business work just wasn't feasible—and now, her data was compromised. Again she called Gina, who told her the same thing. "She said to me, 'The world needs you at your best and you're not at your best.'"

At the same time, Bea was appearing on television and still capturing lots of press. She describes it as living a lie. "I was raining on the inside. I had fallen into the trap of avoiding failure at all costs." That's when she decided it was time.

On April 22, 2016, Bea closed In Your Corner down. Investors and family were disappointed but supportive. And Bea? She expected to feel relieved after closing down. What she felt was profound grief. "I felt like my heart was gasping for air. It's one thing to be dying. It's quite another to be dead. When you're dying, you know it's going to happen, and you're almost ready to get it over with. When you're dead, there's just nothing. I felt dead."

Bea allowed herself six weeks of complete depression. She soon made an important discovery. "Here's the thing they don't tell you when the world is ending. The world is actually much bigger and brighter than you think. When you have your startup, you're so narrowly focused on what you're doing, you miss the world around you. There are a lot more options than you think."

Once Bea rose from her six-week "hiatus from life," she saw all the opportunities in front of her. She started speaking publicly about her failure, and getting requests to do more. She's now working with tech and media companies to provide in-house therapy as part of their perks package; and she's hosting a Web series with Forbes' new digital platform for women. And, in perhaps the most interesting twist of all, those heavily funded competitors called her to come work for them. She took on some consulting, and saw that her business had a lot more going for it than she had given herself credit for. "I was shocked at how much they didn't actually know. It was sort of a reverse impostor syndrome!"

Now, Bea is rebuilding, starting a think tank around mental health called The Difference, based on the concept that the right talk at the right time can make all the difference. A lot of her research is focused on bouncing back from failure, something she hopes more women will learn to be comfortable with.

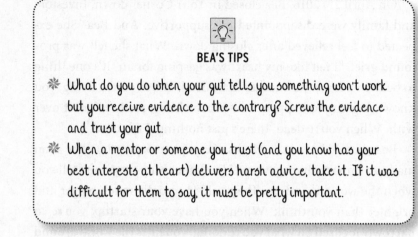

BEA'S TIPS

❋ What do you do when your gut tells you something won't work but you receive evidence to the contrary? Screw the evidence and trust your gut.

❋ When a mentor or someone you trust (and you know has your best interests at heart) delivers harsh advice, take it. If it was difficult for them to say, it must be pretty important.

Find the Good in the Ugliest Times of Your Life

Every one of us will stumble at some point in our careers, but few will suffer a trip-up as publicly as Julie Roehm did.

Moments before Julie Roehm walked into my office to be interviewed for my podcast, I did a little googling. Of course, I was aware of Julie's story—how she was a top executive in the notoriously male-dominated auto industry before she was epically and famously fired from a senior leadership position at Walmart after just ten months for some form of "improper conduct." I wasn't aware of how viciously she was attacked by the press and was horrified at what I discovered. Take a look at some of the headlines from major publications about Julie:

"Unruly Julie and the Scandal That Rocked the Ad World"

"Behind the Rebranding Campaign of Walmart's Scarlet Woman"

"Julie Roehm, Walmart's Psycho Ex-Girlfriend, Wants to Be Your 'Regal Warrior Guru'"

I couldn't imagine coming back from that kind of public vitriol. Yet, here she was walking into my office, head held high.

So what exactly was her "improper conduct"? Julie was hired by Walmart as the senior vice president of marketing communications—and she was specifically hired to fight off the sudden and aggressive rise of the incomparably cool, stylish discount retailer Target. By all accounts, this was a smart hire. After all, Julie was cool and stylish herself, and she had reinvented the brands she'd worked on before. Whether she was successfully branding the Ford Focus for the under-thirty crowd by giving them away to celebrities like P. Diddy, or reinventing Dodge with the sexy "Grab Life by the Horns" tagline, Julie was a risk taker, and her risks usually paid off in a big way. She was exactly what Walmart thought they needed.

So when the darling of the auto industry—an industry that oozed sex and sizzle—picked up her family and moved to Bentonville, Arkansas, where the Walmart headquarters are located, she didn't have the best feeling. She couldn't explain her uneasiness, really—it was just clear that they did business very differently at Walmart than anywhere Julie had been before. Just ten months later she was fired for "improper conduct"—accused of accepting gifts (dinner, a glass of wine . . .) from agency partners. Julie knew the rules, and she followed them as best she could, but you can't accept even a tissue from someone when you work at Walmart. No matter how hard she tried, she felt she was set up to fail. The firing was loud, and it was public—her emails released, photos, and lawsuits and counter-lawsuits galore. It was, by all accounts, a nightmare.

So was this all because Julie was a bold, attractive woman who sold "sexier ideas" than Walmart was ready for? Many thought so. Sergio Zyman, Coca-Cola's former CMO, spoke to Fast Company about a trip he took to meet and counsel Julie after the incident.

"Walmart wanted to wear a pair of high heels, and Julie was high heels," says Zyman, who made marketing history himself with the 1980s New Coke debacle. "But when they put on the high heels, they said, 'No, this is too difficult for me, my feet hurt.' Then the high heels became the problem."

So how did Julie bounce back from this kind of humiliating, public failure? Time, hard work, and most of all, a healthy dose of perspective. During our podcast interview, she told me how she started consulting again and how the longtime close contacts and colleagues she'd had at companies like *Sports Illustrated*, helped her launch her consulting career and a successful business that she ran for five years while she rebuilt her confidence. She was courted by several companies for executive positions, but waited for the perfect fit and ultimately landed a position as chief marketing officer.

What she talked most passionately about was what she learned.

"Carrie," she said, looking at me with an intense clarity. "I learned that culture eats strategy for lunch. I could have been the Michael Jordan of marketing and it wouldn't have mattered there—because it wasn't a culture fit. I did not belong at Walmart—my personal energy, my speed, my style. I could have recognized that immediately, but I ignored my gut warning signs."

That perspective helped her a ton in her career, but it was also the perspective of her son that helped her bounce back. "'Mom,' he said to me. 'If you hadn't taken that job and gone through that, our whole life would have been different. And I like our life.' This is the way to look at the world—you can look back at the ugliest times in your life and turn it around to see what about it made you happy and grateful, and got you where you are today. If you can get through it and find that meaning? You can be better tomorrow."

JULIE'S TIPS

❋ When joining a company, remember that company culture eats strategy for lunch. No matter how good you are at your job, if you're not finding the culture to be a fit for you, your work will be a struggle.

❋ Take the ugliest time in your life and ask yourself, "How can I be grateful for that?" Find something worthwhile you learned from that experience.

PLANT SEEDS OF PASSION IN YOUR CAREER:
A CASE STUDY WITH LISA FERIA, PRESIDENT OF STRAY DOG CAPITAL

Growing up in San Juan, Puerto Rico, Lisa Feria was parented by a mother with a very specific philosophy—one that Lisa says shaped her career and her life. She called it "planting seeds."

When Lisa was a child, her mother would expose her to dozens of different people, classes, locations, and experiences. The theory was that you would never know what your passions were if you weren't exposed to them. Even if Lisa wasn't sure if she'd like a class, her mom would "plant seeds" by having Lisa try new things. She didn't have to stick with things that didn't resonate, but when she would find something, they would invest hard in making sure that those were the seeds that were cultivated.

Lisa attended college in the States—studying chemical engineering at Georgia Tech. After some time working as an engineer, Lisa fell in love with marketing, and decided to enroll in school for her MBA.

After her MBA, Lisa secured a job at P&G. Lisa felt this was an obvious choice. "This was a learning company. I was exposed to so many different areas of senior leadership. I was able to figure out what I loved because of this exposure—just like when I was a kid and trying a million different things."

Lisa was tapped to head up the Puffs business at P&G. During her time there, Lisa kept her eye on the Greenpeace and PETA Web sites—they frequently called out brands for animal testing, and had recently run a campaign against Kleenex, a competitor of Puffs. While Lisa was doing her research, she came across a video called "Meet Your Meat"— all about the cruel treatment of animals in factory farms. Lisa describes this as a turning point in her life. Lisa couldn't "unsee" what she had seen.

She started experimenting with small changes based on what she had read and viewed about the treatment of animals. First, she became a vegetarian. But she felt like it wasn't enough. Soon, she became a vegan. At P&G, she began to educate people about a vegan lifestyle. It was really great because she felt like she was a normal, non-hippie person educating people about veganism. P&G catering services received and acted on feedback from Lisa in order to offer vegan-friendly options. Still, the PETA and Greenpeace info was keeping her up at night. And the reality was, she could do everything personally to help, but professionally, she was working for a company that tested products on an-imals, and that no longer became an option for her.

Lisa was positive that she could find a job that would unite her professional and philosophical beliefs. She started looking, and she found a job in the unlikeliest of places: Kansas.

Stray Dog Capital is a venture capitalist firm that be-lieves all animals can live in peaceful coexistence. They provide early-stage, groundbreaking businesses with the capital and support to grow their businesses and shift away from an animal-based economy. And they were looking for someone to lead the firm.

Lisa had no VC experience but she leaped at the oppor-tunity, moving from Cincinnati to Kansas. This decision, which was entirely gut-based, was made with the support of her family, who had all become vegan over time with Lisa. As for being a VC? That she learned by doing—but it was easier because she was so passionate about the work. "The magic happens when you are able to match and over-lay your personal beliefs and passion with your professional skills and abilities."

Congratulations! You've now learned the basics—*and* how to better identify your gut instincts—helping you understand the importance of saying yes when you mean yes, and no when you mean no. You've also learned about the various ways one can be an entrepreneur—and that, like most things, it's not all black and white. Entrepreneurship isn't for everyone, but an entrepreneurial spirit can benefit everyone. In this section, we've faced our worst fear and experienced failure—but we've also seen the benefits that failing can bring us. It's time to bring us home. We now have the tools to succeed. But sometimes, real life gets in the way.

First, there's the whole confidence issue you've likely been facing your whole life. You may not have the confidence to believe you can get there. If you find yourself saying, "Oh, that's easy for her to say . . . she's (insert reason she is better than you here)," you need a swift dose of part 3. Even without the confidence issue, we face the real-life challenges that make it easy for us to be held back—after all, we're the ones who have to spend the extra half hour (okay, hour) getting ready in the morning, the ones who have to birth the babies we want, the ones who have to worry about whether or not we are "likeable" enough in the workplace.

This is what we talk about in part 3: Work It Practically. I'll see you there.

PART 3

Work It Practically:
Ways to Work It in
Every Part of Your Life

CHAPTER 11

Crack Your Confidence Code

IT'S INTERESTING, WHEN I look at all the previous chapters of this book—whether it's how to get the right job, or how to learn how to trust your instincts—it all comes down to one thing: having confidence in yourself. As someone who has struggled with this my entire life, I can tell you that the only thing that's ever truly worked for me is channeling the old biblical adage "Act as if." If I act as if I am confident, I will become confident. Such was the case in 2012, when I was placed in a role that required confidence, and somehow I felt none.

After a series of intense conversations about our goals, it was decided. Dave was going to raise funds and launch a startup called Likeable Local—a technology platform designed to help small businesses as opposed to the large clients we currently worked with. Meanwhile, I would step into the CEO role at Likeable Media and run our existing business myself.

I do remember feeling excited about this prospect at the time.

But when the actual transition moment came, I was in total panic. I had spent my first entrepreneurial years executing every vision that Dave had. Now, I had to have my own vision—and I wasn't sure if I was capable of that. I remember the first team address I made. When I looked out at the faces of the employees I had personally hired through the years, I knew they saw something in me that I couldn't see in myself. And I knew I had to trust that and "Act as if."

Those first few weeks as CEO were fun. I got to take a fresh look at the business, dig deep in all of the data, and learn. I compiled the results of what I'd found. And suddenly, it wasn't so fun anymore.

Life for a social media agency in 2013 wasn't what it was in those magical early years. The social media space had become much more crowded. PR firms now offered social media, creative agencies were offering it as well, and meanwhile, brands were hiring internally instead of using agencies. In addition to all of this, we had built our agency in a time when tech companies like Buddy Media and Wildfire were getting insane valuations and selling for hundreds of millions to giants like Google and Salesforce—and at the time we had felt very strongly that we needed to prioritize growth over all else in order to live and grow in the tech wave we were riding. Thanks to that, we had been one of the fastest-growing companies in the country, but profitability was not something we thought about often at that time. We were low on cash, high on staff, with a product that was no longer unique, in a competitive marketplace. Hooray for my new job!

So what do you do when you feel unprepared to handle a challenge that seems so overwhelming you can't even breathe? You act as if you know what to do, and you do it.

As a business owner, I had no other choice. I couldn't quit and find a new job. I couldn't (or wouldn't) shut the doors. So the only option left was to step up and set a plan . . . and whatever plan I set,

I had to own it with a confidence that I hadn't felt since my early sales career.

I made two key decisions:

1. I was going to prioritize profitability over growth.
2. I was going to narrow our services to be even more niche than just a "social media agency," which was now a common thing.

Regarding profitability, I put the following saying on a Post-it note on my computer screen:

> "Revenue is vanity. Profit is sanity."

Now that I had decided my first move was to get profitable, I had to set a strategy for how I was going to grow. There were two options: either I could start taking lots of different types of business and become a full-service agency, or I could scale a productized version of a single service we offered. I could take one thing, do it really well, and do it over and over again for lots of different companies.

I chose the latter for a few reasons. First, I knew that the staff I had was excellent at social media content creation, and that I'd have to do very little to ramp up a plan. Second, I saw an opening.

I knew that the second large agencies got involved in social media content creation, the prices would go way up. I knew that internal hires generally would be "social media managers" and "community managers," and that actual creatives still preferred agency environments. I knew that video and multimedia content was on the rise—and I knew that the social networks were under a tremendous amount of pressure to monetize, and new ad units would be introduced at a rapid-fire pace. Lastly, I knew that we were seen as true experts in this space—we had a long history of doing great work, and a level of credibility that couldn't be ignored.

I created a three-step process called Content Cubed, where we created social media content and distributed it using social advertising, all based on listening to data across the social Web. We used insights to explain why our content would perform better, and it always did. We removed every other service that we offered. We changed our brand promise to be about offering faster service, from the smartest in social, with likeability guaranteed. Now more of a smart social media production house, we owned a lane where few competed. As a result, we doubled in size, and became more profitable than most agencies. No big deal, right?

Did all of this happen because I suddenly decided to be confident? Hardly. In many ways, we succeeded because I made a very tough but educated decision to steer the company in a new direction based on looking at the state of the business itself. This would take talent and an incredible amount of hard work, and I knew we had enough of both to make this vital turnaround. But having confidence mattered as well. Had I not been confident enough to make this bold decision, our competence as a company would have been irrelevant. You can't deliver a new concept like this without fully believing in yourself. And even when you don't believe in yourself, you'd still better act like you do if you want to get anywhere.

That's why we don't only need confidence when we feel worthy of it. Seeing our company's bank account hit seven figures for the first time—an undeniable metric that meant my decision was a success—gave me an immense boost of confidence. But more important, we need confidence most when we *don't* feel worthy. In my case, that was when I was sitting at my desk, three months into the CEO role, wondering how the hell I was going to save this company from certain death.

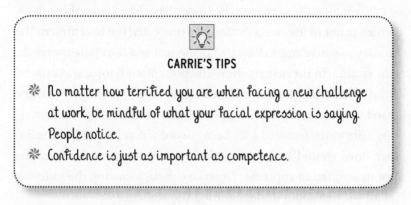

CARRIE'S TIPS

❊ No matter how terrified you are when facing a new challenge at work, be mindful of what your facial expression is saying. People notice.

❊ Confidence is just as important as competence.

Focus on Learning and Adapting, Not Looking Good

When I think about women I admire who exude confidence, I think of one of the top CMOs I know, Lisa Baird. Lisa was recently named one of the Top 50 Most Innovative CMOs by Business Insider, and I get why: she's taken Team USA to new heights through the brilliant marketing of the United States Olympic Committee. But Lisa's career wasn't always about sports—in fact, most of it was totally unrelated.

Lisa had a successful career in marketing for a number of different industries—including beauty, automotive, and tech. Her very first job in sports marketing was a big one: when she joined the NFL as the senior vice president of marketing and consumer products.

Having never worked in sports before, Lisa found that she had to overcome her intimidation around learning about a new industry. She remembers when she had her first meeting with the NFL team owners. "Team owners are knowledgeable, and they're highly invested. There was no way that I'd know more about sports, or even potentially sports marketing, than they would." Lisa knew she couldn't win that battle, but she had an idea.

Throughout Lisa's career, her focus has always been the same—which is not to use her "opinion as a marketer, but to represent the audience you're marketing to." If she just stuck to that approach, she could win the owners over. The presentation topic was around youth marketing for the NFL. Using the same philosophy that she used in other industries, Lisa produced a video to play at the meeting. The video featured kids being asked where *they* think the Super Bowl should be held this year. When Lisa was finished, the room erupted in applause. "It wasn't about knowing the industry at all—it was about understanding the audience."

When you change industries within your career, it's natural that you might feel a little less confident. Keep an open attitude and try to learn as much as you can, and you'll be a pro in no time.

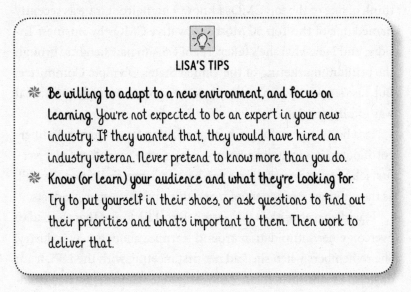

LISA'S TIPS

❋ **Be willing to adapt to a new environment, and focus on learning.** You're not expected to be an expert in your new industry. If they wanted that, they would have hired an industry veteran. Never pretend to know more than you do.

❋ **Know (or learn) your audience and what they're looking for.** Try to put yourself in their shoes, or ask questions to find out their priorities and what's important to them. Then work to deliver that.

Start a Confidence Log

Sometimes, you're really confident in yourself, and then you're presented an opportunity that pushes you way outside of your comfort zone. When Kristen Durkin was recruited by Facebook, she had to treat it as if it were a joke. "I was humbled, I was flattered, but I could not possibly think that they would want to hire me. I just wouldn't allow myself to think that I could get this job." Of course, when Kristen was offered the product manager position, she was shocked and said yes immediately.

When you start at Facebook, you're working with the best of the best. They're disciplined, they've sold companies, they're incredibly successful, and Kristen was intimidated. She spent the first six months of her tenure with Facebook in the bathroom, crying. "I didn't feel that I had any right to speak up in meetings. I didn't feel that my former work life stacked up at all with my peers." It felt like there was a dark cloud over her.

The other dark cloud? The fact that she worked at an organization led by Sheryl Sandberg. Sheryl was all about "leaning in," and the only thing Kristen could think about? "Leaning the fuck back. Do I really deserve a seat at this table? I don't think so."

Ultimately, Kristen gained confidence, not only from within, but because she had leaders at the company explicitly telling her to "step up and sit at the damn table." She recalls going into a business review meeting early headed up by Andrew Bosworth, a VP and tech whiz known to most as "Boz." The meeting was held in a room with couches, which was typical of Facebook. Behind the couches were benches along the perimeter of the room. Kristen took the seat she thought she should—on one of the perimeter benches outside the group, even though the couches weren't full. Boz, who did not know her name at the time, immediately approached her and said, "What's your name, what are you working on, and come sit at the couch." This was a key moment for Kristen. Not only was it so embarrassing to see how evident her lack of confidence was, she knew Boz was right. Why on earth *shouldn't* she be sitting on the couch?

For the rest of her first year at Facebook, almost all of her professional development was focused on building confidence. "Almost every comment I made was about people being smarter than I was, because I was so intimidated. I'd say, 'You probably know this better than I do,' and that just made me look dumb. Ultimately, I had to learn to say it in my head, swallow it, and forget about it."

She also took some specific actions to help her get over the intimidation factor. For example, she started keeping a "confidence log," recording who was in the room when she felt intimidated, what was the subject matter being discussed, and did she work through it. The log allowed Kristen to see when and where she was hesitating to speak up, and recognizing these factors and patterns allowed her to work through them. When you're accountable to writing things in a journal, you pay much more attention—think of it like Weight Watchers, but for confidence. It's improved her confidence tenfold, and her performance as a result. Best of all, as a result of this hard work, Kristen has been promoted at Facebook, and is not only more confident, she's much happier, too.

KRISTEN'S TIPS

❋ When you're intimidated by those around you, resist the urge to put yourself down. It won't do you or your confidence any favors.

> ❋ Every time you feel inadequate, ask yourself, "Why?" Write down the reason you felt that way, where you were, who you were with, and what you were doing at the time. Note patterns and address them.

A Little Bit of Worry Can Help You Do a Better Job

While Kristen is now part of the team running the show at Facebook, the rest of us are just hanging out on there, seeing what's happening around us. One of the people who always shows up in my Facebook feed is Carla Sosenko, my good friend and executive editor at *Entertainment Weekly*. The reason is the algorithm: Facebook knows which content I like the best, and Carla's updates are hysterical. Carla is so hilariously self-deprecating, despite the fact that she is one of the most successful women I know.

When Carla was the managing editor at *Life & Style*, she felt on top of her game. She knew everything and anything about the job. She was comfortable, and quite happy. When her boss gave notice and suggested that she apply for her current job, that of executive editor, Carla thought she was nuts. "I'd never been an executive editor. I'd never done anything like that before. I said yes—but I had absolutely no confidence in my abilities."

Years later, when that same boss moved over to *Time Out New York* as editor in chief, she wanted to bring Carla on as deputy editor. Carla felt almost the exact same way—she hadn't been a deputy editor before, and worried that she would choke.

"Every single morning before I went to work, I'd have an anxiety attack. Looking back, it was all about being terrified that I wouldn't live up to expectations. Could I really do this job well?"

Carla worked her ass off, keeping her head down, and doing everything that was asked of her. In the process, she became an excellent deputy editor, and was indispensable to the editor in chief. Not only was she now officially the right-hand woman to the person at the top, but she became the go-to person to the team, building relationships at every level.

Soon thereafter, the editor in chief gave notice and once again offered Carla her job. "It felt like the most severe case of déjà vu."

Her first thought? "Hell. No."

How could she handle being in the top position at the magazine? She had only just gained confidence as a deputy editor. But turning it down would send a signal that Carla also might want to leave—and she knew that she didn't. So, she decided to bite the bullet and said yes.

What happened next was even more terrifying for Carla—the anxiety she felt as a deputy editor multiplied by a million. "I fell apart. The thought that I wouldn't be good was totally paralyzing to me."

Somehow, she managed to get into work every day. At first, she found it disorienting. "I wanted to know everything there was to know as an editor in chief by my first day on the job. That was impossible. So I took it day by day, learning, and making mistakes."

Little by little, Carla gained confidence, and one day finally was able to call herself a "great editor in chief." What does she credit for her eventual acknowledgment of her success? "I honestly think it's being a little bit insecure. You work harder when you're terrified that you won't be good. If I weren't insecure, wouldn't that mean I didn't care?"

In Carla's mind, the moment she stops worrying, she might stop being motivated to do a great job. So nowadays, instead of trying to force herself *not* to worry, her goal is to manage her worry level so it doesn't become so all-consuming that it negatively impacts her health and peace of mind anymore.

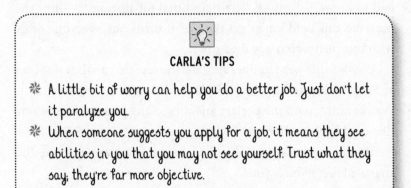

CARLA'S TIPS

✳ A little bit of worry can help you do a better job. Just don't let it paralyze you.

✳ When someone suggests you apply for a job, it means they see abilities in you that you may not see yourself. Trust what they say; they're far more objective.

Own Your Insecurities

As Carla will tell you, a little insecurity can be the key to success and security. I discovered this during one of my first interviews for my podcast, *All the Social Ladies*. It was with one of the most confident women I know: Sallie Krawcheck.

Known as one of the most senior women on Wall Street, Sallie had served as president of the Global Wealth and Investment Management division of Bank of America. She currently is the CEO and cofounder of Ellevest, a digital financial advisor to women. You'd think, with that kind of background, Sallie would be sharing stories about money management in one of the earlier chapters. And, of course, she has lots of advice in that area. However, something she'd said during our first podcast interview had stuck with me far longer than any financial advice she could have given me.

"Carrie, when I worked at Sanford Bernstein they used to hire *for* insecurity. Not for a lack of it, but for some of it. Insecurity can be an amazing motivator. It's not necessarily a bad thing."

When you see Sallie, this gorgeous tall blonde, perfectly dressed and the epitome of success, you don't exactly think insecure. But I had to know, if Sanford Bernstein hired for insecurity—how the heck did this bold leader get the gig? It turns out, everyone deals with insecurity. Here's Sallie's story.

When Sallie went to interview for the research analyst position at Sanford Bernstein, she had planned it perfectly. Perfect hair. Perfect outfit. And the perfect answers to any potential questions that could be shot her way.

The hiring manager, John, said to her: "You've had quite the charmed life, haven't you?"

Sallie was aware that everything about her looked like she was a "member of the Upper East Side Junior League." She had it all: the perfect apartment, husband, baby, and certainly the look. "Everything about me screamed secure and privileged."

At first, she laughed it off. When he said something about it again, she got a little annoyed. By the third time that he implied that she was basically a "Park Avenue WASP," she decided it was time to set him straight.

"Look, John, you may think I've had everything handed to me, but you don't know me at all."

She proceeded to tell him the story of her first marriage—and how the man she'd been so deeply in love with had had an affair with her friend. She told him how stupid she felt that she was so sure he was faithful, that she didn't think to ask. So sure that when she'd return home and find the curtains had been closed after she'd left them open, and that hairs that weren't hers were on her bed, she'd just assumed that no, this couldn't be happening to her. Their life was too perfect—so she'd simply keep "forgetting" to ask him. When she finally thought to ask him and he fessed up, she could remember the world "literally" shaking. She dropped down to 108 pounds, and was vomiting in between meetings at her first job. Her social life imploded since this was an affair with a friend, and it got real awkward, real fast.

It turns out, Sallie's entire image was all about coming back from that horrible insecurity—she was going to create the life she wanted even though she wasn't "good enough" for her first husband. She needed to "work harder to not fail next time."

She walked out of the interview convinced it was over. She was hired the next day.

Like Sanford Bernstein, Sallie sees insecurity—as long as it's not paralyzing—to ultimately be a good thing. "It's a good thing to feel like you need to get up earlier than the boys to make sure you're prepared for the meeting. It's a good thing to challenge yourself to be better. That's what Sanford looked for in me as a hire, and that's part of what's made me so successful today." If you start owning your worries and your insecurities like Carla and Sallie have, rather than letting them own you, you can turn them into amazing motivators for success.

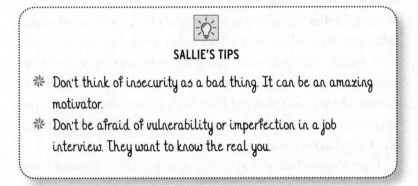

SALLIE'S TIPS

❋ Don't think of insecurity as a bad thing. It can be an amazing motivator.

❋ Don't be afraid of vulnerability or imperfection in a job interview. They want to know the real you.

CHAPTER 12

Hack Your Highlight Reel

WHEN YOU WORK in social media, part of your job is using the tools that you offer to your clients. Part of that process is crafting a "personal brand" for yourself. But part of it is simply reading and absorbing what's happening around you.

It's said that "comparison is the thief of joy," and social media takes that expression to a whole other level. For me, it wasn't the perfectly sculpted bodies flying across Instagram, it wasn't the perfect re-creation of Pinterest craft projects by neighborhood moms, and it wasn't that kid from high school who was flying in his own private jet around the world. For me, the thief of my joy was Gary Vaynerchuk.

Gary Vaynerchuk was already a successful entrepreneur when he started his agency VaynerMedia in 2009. And it was evident from the start that he was going to be successful with that, too. He already had a significant following, and, of course, it was right around the time that I became CEO that Gary kicked it into high gear. He started a daily Web series documenting his life. He started keynoting huge events. And he landed a huge story on the front page of the *New York Times* business section.

As a businessperson, Gary was everything I wasn't. He was all about putting himself out there—exuding a confidence that might have seemed ridiculous in the past. He was all about the "hustle"— showing himself working sometimes twenty-four-hour days on social media. He cursed and he was uneducated, and he quickly became the darling of Fortune 500 CMOs. He. Was. Everywhere.

Soon, I couldn't go onto a social media feed without seeing Gary pop up in some way—after all, he's posting content that gets shared around the clock. And the thing is, I didn't even dislike him. Sure, I thought half of what he said was bonkers, and I didn't understand why he valued working 24/7 to "avoid regret," but mostly, I felt like he really understood the concept of great content, and I admired his salesmanship.

But mostly, I felt like I just was nowhere near as good.

For every piece of content I produced, Gary would produce ten. When I was checking my feed on one of my ten thousand trips to the orthodontist, there was Gary, out for drinks with a client. As I was being incredibly careful with head count and payroll, Gary was talking about hiring his six *hundredth* employee. It tapped into every insecurity I had—I had no desire to hustle twenty-four hours a day, and I had no money to hire a billion employees, and I was downright unwilling to record every moment of my life and turn it into a docuseries. If this was what worked in my industry—well, shit, maybe I was in the wrong industry.

The more Gary grew, the more it felt like I shrank. One day, I was thumbing through quotes to use for a team meeting, and I came across a quote from a pastor. Normally, I quoted great business leaders at meetings, so this was not something I'd usually pay attention to, but it stopped me dead in my tracks when I read it.

"The reason we struggle with insecurity is because we compare our behind-the-scenes with everyone else's highlight reel."

Of course. I saw Gary through the lens of his highlight reel on social media, which presented the best of the best about him. I knew nothing of his real life behind the scenes. And the same goes for everyone else on social media who seemed thinner, smarter, or better than I was. We are all just trying to present the best versions of ourselves. And we should—in fact, it's an immense opportunity to use these channels to create a clear and strong image of who you want to be. But in that process we must remember that we're all showing our highlight reels, and living our real, messy, and wonderfully imperfect lives behind the scenes. Try not to compare your behind-the-scenes to someone else's highlight reel; it's comparing apples to oranges and it won't get you anywhere.

CARRIE'S TIPS

❋ When building your career or your business, try to put your blinders on. Comparison is the thief of joy.

❋ When you feel envious of someone, remember that you have no idea what goes on beyond what you see about them in the media or online. Everyone has their own issues and trials to grapple with and none of us is perfect.

Turn Intimidation into Inspiration

I wasn't the only one getting psyched out by social media experts like Gary Vaynerchuk on the Internet. When Vanessa Sain-Dieguez was approached by someone at Hilton to lead the company's social media in 2010, she was apprehensive. She was an e-commerce manager for a single Hilton hotel at the time, and while she used social media locally, she had no experience building a global strategy. After all, social media was still entirely new territory for brands.

The first thing she did when considering the position was initiate some serious social media research. She dove into Twitter and Facebook and found countless updates from social media experts. She felt totally intimidated. "I was watching videos from speakers on the global social economy, and I was reading tweets from women who literally wrote the book on social media." The result? Vanessa felt unprepared for the job and questioned whether or not she had the right skills to get the job done—and with that, whether or not she should be taking it on.

It was only when Vanessa reframed this process in her mind that she was able not only to accept the position, but to thrive in it. Vanessa saw the highlight reels that she was watching of other thought leaders as inspiration versus competition. She was completely capable and didn't have to have all the answers to take the job. Instead, she says, "I decided to take a leap and build my parachute while in the air." And in that process, Vanessa was instrumental in creating one of the most successfully branded Twitter handles in history—@HiltonSuggests—a Twitter handle that acts as a global concierge to travelers in need, regardless of whether or not they are Hilton guests. Any question you might have about a city you were traveling to, you could just tweet it to @HiltonSuggests for their thoughts. Vanessa built the model to staff this account and grew it to 100+ contributors worldwide—all with suggestions at the ready. This concept of Social Customer Care was led by Vanessa, and it never would have happened if she had let the highlight reel hold her back.

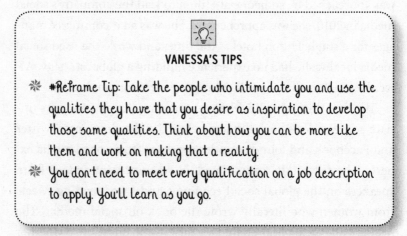

VANESSA'S TIPS

❋ #Reframe Tip: Take the people who intimidate you and use the qualities they have that you desire as inspiration to develop those same qualities. Think about how you can be more like them and work on making that a reality.

❋ You don't need to meet every qualification on a job description to apply. You'll learn as you go.

Learn How to Brag Better

It seems to me that there are two issues with the highlight reel—learning how to not compare your successes with others', and creating your own narrative to help yourself look like the success that you truly are. To address exactly these challenges, one need not look further than Meredith Fineman, founder and CEO of FinePoint, a personal branding firm. Meredith noticed one very important fact about most of the women she met: no one knew how to talk about themselves.

Meredith would have young women come into her office and say that their accomplishments were stupid. At networking events, she found herself hopping into conversations to explain all of the amazing things her friends were doing—because they wouldn't dare say it about themselves. And she would represent a lot of

CEOs and founders who felt a tremendous amount of discomfort telling their stories. Meredith pivoted her company to be focused on teaching women and girls how to self-promote.

Despite the inclination not to promote ourselves, and despite our feelings about other people constantly promoting themselves online, learning how to talk about yourself and share your successes is essential. As Meredith explains, "If a great product falls in the woods and nobody hears about it, you just have a dead tree in the woods." We have a responsibility to promote the work that we're doing. Why do we find it so hard?

Well, first, we're busy looking at the highlight reels of others and feeling inadequate. When we are accustomed to using platforms like Instagram that literally photoshop our lives to look better, we also become trained to believe these images of others are their reality. When Meredith feels herself getting jealous, she asks herself if she actually wants to be that person in that moment with that exact accomplishment. Ninety-nine percent of the time, she doesn't. Chances are, neither will you.

Aside from highlight-reel envy, something holding us back is the simple fact that the media (including the social media audience) judge women on metrics that it doesn't use to judge men. As an example, Meredith remembers a time when she attended a gala. She was standing with a friend who is a well-known on-air personality when another woman walked up to say that she was a big fan. Out of nowhere, the woman asked, "Have you ever considered getting some vocal coaching?" Meredith's friend looked at the woman and said, "No, I think my voice is fine." Afterward, Meredith asked how often that sort of thing happened, and her friend responded, "All the time." This type of unsolicited critical feedback is something every woman deals with every day.

Meredith's company's mission is to help women brag better. The trick to that is getting excited about your work. What if you can't be excited about yourself? "Just pretend," advises Meredith. "But really, there's no reason not to be genuinely excited about what you've done."

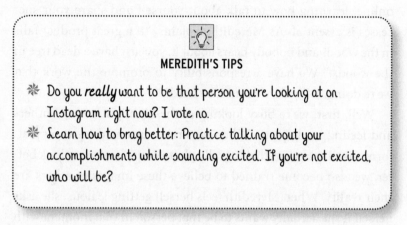

MEREDITH'S TIPS

❋ Do you *really* want to be that person you're looking at on Instagram right now? I vote no.

❋ Learn how to brag better: Practice talking about your accomplishments while sounding excited. If you're not excited, who will be?

EXERCISE FOUR

Create Your Highlight Reel with the Total Stranger Test

A highlight reel is the image you give off to other people. In the old days, this was about how you presented yourself in person, but in our current climate the highlight reel is most obviously shown in your online footprint—both when people google your name and in your social profiles.

I'm going to need you to summon some courage right now—I'm going to ask you to step out of your comfort zone a bit. I want you to ask your friends to show your social profiles to someone who they know, but you *don't*. Ask them to scroll through your feeds, and describe you in three words—ideally none based on physical

*Here's an example of what people have
said about my highlight reel.*

appearance (i.e., pretty, tall, cute smile, etc.). Have as many people
do this as you can bear—and write every adjective in the circle on
the next page.

These are your truest answers to your current-day highlight
reel—because they are how strangers perceive you. This, in addition to your "googled" self, is the most authentic and real reflec-
tion of your highlight reel.

So, looking at your circle, how do the adjectives used to describe
you make you feel? If bad, or even neutral, it's time to work on your
own highlight reel. You might be thinking—I'm private, I have no
reason to do this. However, I would argue that everyone needs to
have some form of highlight reel in today's day and age. At a time

when 60 percent of employers are openly revealing that they use social networking sites to research job candidates (check out CareerBuilders' 2016 social media recruitment survey for the full report), it's important to have some form of highlight reel. Sometimes we are held back by our fear of seeming arrogant. Sometimes we are held back from doing so because we're so psyched out by others' successes online. There are dozens of excuses, and I've heard them all—let's just shed our insecurities once and for all and WORK IT.

CHAPTER 13

Learn to Love Your Look

WHILE WE'RE ON the subject of how you look on your social media feeds—let's talk about how you look IRL. Your highlight reel contains your best looks—but what about your everyday appearance?

Most women who write books and talk about working a look probably would feature lots of tips on how they developed their own style. Me? I'm going to tell you about the worst fashion "don't" of my career.

I was still early in my CEO days and I was now hours away from leaving for our first family trip to Europe. In my typical plane gear, yoga pants with a hoodie and a schlumpy ponytail, I came in to take a few meetings before jetting off to a Parisian paradise with my family. One meeting was with another agency CEO, Margi Booth. Margi had sold her agency and was now working for the holding company sourcing potential future acquisitions. Since I had no intention of being acquired, I had no problem taking the meeting in my yoga pants and ponytail. In fact, much of my shtick is that I generally wear a ponytail and little makeup.

Dave was big into the book *Mastering the Rockefeller Habits*, which was all about putting up public scorecards of your business's goals, financials, and growth. When he ran our agency, all of the numbers were up everywhere. I had slowly been reducing this practice as I felt it made employees nervous. I started putting the preprinted whiteboards in the "war room" in the back. When Margi entered with her holding company's CEO, all of my regular conference rooms were full, so I had my assistant, Jo, place them in my least favorite room: the war room.

Margi walked in, perfectly coiffed and beautiful. Her silver hair was worn in a short stylish cut—the kind I'd always wanted but never had been able to maintain. Her jewelry was bold and bright, and she had the perfect shade of lipstick for her skin tone. When I bounced into the war room in my yoga pants, I suddenly wished I was better prepared.

I watched as Margi's eyes scanned the room, and saw them land on the whiteboard—which had my "goal" of hitting 10 percent profitability—a paltry number by agency standards, but a good number for me, since I was just rebuilding the company's profitability in the first place.

"Ten percent, huh? Gosh, I remember those days. I operated with tiny margins until it was time to sell. Then I sold and learned how to *really* be profitable. I remember wishing I had done that years prior—I had no idea why I *always* didn't operate that way!"

I think my skin turned the actual color of eggplant while I stammered about how I was in the middle of reinventing the agency, and "Oh my, these numbers are old," and "Oh yes, I love profitability."

Standing there looking schlumpy and feeling schlumpy, I knew that this was the last meeting I'd take in yoga pants and a frizzy ponytail. I slunk off to Paris, and managed to enjoy the week with my family.

But when I came back, I took the metrics off the wall wanting to burn them, actually. All the while, I kept thinking about Margi. I couldn't even adequately evaluate her feedback around the financials—not when I was feeling so vulnerable about my unpolished appearance. So I decided I'd ask her again.

I called Margi, and set up lunch to thank her for the feedback on the profitability and to ask her some questions about how she built such an incredible business. This time I was dressed to impress, and Margi was thrilled that she helped me. We became fast friends, and sure enough, she joined my FAB PAB.

CARRIE'S TIPS

❋ At work, always dress like you have an important meeting to attend.

❋ Bad first impressions can be tough to overcome, but if you want to forge a connection with the person, it's worth making the effort to try to turn their first impression of you around.

Find Your Signature Style and Work It!

When I think of a woman whose signature style I admire, I think of influencer, entrepreneur, and digital correspondent Sarah Evans. Sarah was well known on Twitter, even in her earliest days as a director of communications at a community college. She became a rising star in the social world, mostly known as a tech-obsessed journalist who was rooted in community building. She caught the entrepreneurial bug in 2009 and launched Sevans Strategy, which enabled her to act as a digital correspondent and consultant on all things tech for companies like Walmart and PayPal.

Sarah always had poor vision, and consistently wore either contacts or glasses ever since she was a little girl. As she was growing her business, she began her search for a look that was "memorable." She saw that the "geek chic" culture was on the rise, and she picked out a bold, square-shaped pair of frames for her latest pair of glasses. People had a *lot* of opinions.

"People loved the glasses. They hated the glasses. In reality, I didn't care whether they liked them or didn't. I cared that I made people notice."

As time went on, Sarah pushed the boundaries with her glasses, picking the biggest, boldest frames she could find. Some might think Sarah's glasses were silly. In reality, they were anything but.

As a digital correspondent for media companies, Sarah was often on the red carpet, live-streaming celebrity interviews. She found that her glasses made her interesting and memorable, and the crazier her glasses were, the more willing celebrities were to talk to her.

Suddenly, so were eyewear brands.

When Transitions Lenses called Sarah about a partnership, she was unsure. She remembered Transitions from when she was a kid, and she wasn't sure that they represented her tech-savvy brand. As soon as she spoke to them, she learned that they were at the epicenter of technology, particularly with their light-reactive lenses. Sarah signed on as a brand ambassador. It was a mutually beneficial partnership.

If Sarah felt lucky to have found the perfect eyewear brand to partner with, you can imagine her reaction when a social network launched the ability to create content entirely through eyewear.

In 2016, Snapchat redefined their mission and company: they

were no longer a social network. They were a camera company called Snap Inc. Their first release? Spectacles—sunglasses that could film Snapchat videos with the press of a button. Sarah contacted Snapchat to see if she could replace the lenses in her Spectacles with Transitions lenses—blending her brand partnership with the latest in social media technology. The answer was absolutely, prescriptions could be incorporated. Sarah worked with her Transitions team to install lenses in her Spectacles, and voilà— the first prescription pair of Spectacles in the world was born. All thanks to Sarah and her commitment to her signature style.

Sarah gets requests from friends all the time asking about how they can capitalize on something like she did. Sarah remains firm in her approach. "You need to dress the way *you* want and not worry about what anyone else thinks." Of course, right afterward she says, "How you look and what you wear forms people's opinions about you and that's important." She laughs at that contradiction . . . but brings it home with the following words of wisdom: "Your style needs to be your own. If it's authentic, the perception from people will be perfect. Mark Zuckerberg wears his gray T-shirts and hoodies every day—it's his signature style. People know him for it, and it's authentic to who he is."

SARAH'S TIPS

❋ Find a look that is memorable. People can hate it or love it—as long as they remember it.

❋ Your style doesn't have to be zany, but it does have to be your own. Find something distinctive even if it's simple.

Dare to Be Outrageous

Another big fan of statement eyewear is my former employee, and now senior social media manager at Grubhub, Mallorie Rosenbluth. Although she's worn her glasses for her entire professional career, that's not what defines her signature style. If you saw Mallorie walking down the street, you'd definitely recognize her. Her hair is a bright shade of pink, and has been that way throughout the most formative years of her career.

From the time she was little, Mallorie was drawn to the color pink. Nature or nurture, she can't be sure . . . all she knew was, she always wanted pink hair. Once she graduated from college, she wanted to dye the tips of her hair, but began working at a conservative company, so she held off. What did she do instead? "I decorated my *entire* apartment in pink decor. Pink kitchen table and chairs, pink couch, pink bedroom . . . it was the *best!*"

As Mallorie grew in her career, she felt she had the credibility to start experimenting with her hair. Once she had a few years of marketing and sales experience under her belt, she transitioned into a more creative role, and decided to get more creative with her appearance as well. She started with pink tips, getting bolder and bolder until her entire head was an electric pink color.

As Mallorie's employer at the time, I remember thinking that this definitely helped her stand out. But looking back, I wasn't sure if I would have hired her if she had interviewed with the fully pinked-out coif. But Mallorie says that now it's easier to get jobs because of her hairstyle.

"In a lot of ways, I think it helped me stand out. Who forgets the girl with pink hair, right? It's also a great conversation starter. I was always introduced to potential partners at my last job like this: 'I'm joined by Mallorie, our brand director, you should see her hair, you'd love it!' Having hot pink hair be a conversation starter on the subway is creepy, but having it be a conversation starter in the professional world is great. I had an icebreaker right on top of my head."

Mallorie also credits her pink hair for saving her from some potentially horrendous interviews. Her hair is showcased in her LinkedIn picture, which immediately weeds out anyone who wouldn't accept her because of her hair. In addition, Mallorie stresses that maintaining a professional look when you have an outrageous signature style is essential. "The stigma that punks or party girls are the ones with crazy hues is not what I embrace. I haven't become a stereotype. I can still speak at conferences, present to my CEO, and represent my organization during interviews professionally with my pink hair. I'm not showing up in my Doc Martens and band tees."

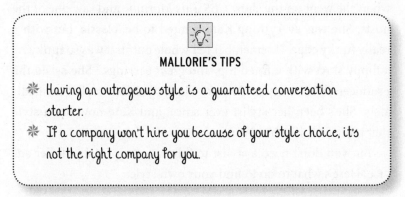

MALLORIE'S TIPS

❋ Having an outrageous style is a guaranteed conversation starter.

❋ If a company won't hire you because of your style choice, it's not the right company for you.

Four Steps to Creating Your Own Style

For many, it's impossible to believe that Kate White, former editor in chief of *Cosmo*, would have been on earth for a single moment of her life without a signature style. But actually, fashion didn't always come easy to Kate.

While she had "a bit of a flair" in high school, Kate says she lost it along the way, because when she got to the working world, she really felt at a loss. Kate remembers when she was at *Working Woman* magazine, she consulted with a stylist. She tried a bunch of things on, and found some nice suits, but she never really felt like herself in them. When she was offered the editor in chief job at *Cosmopolitan* magazine, someone very high up in communications at Hearst suggested she head to Bergdorf Goodman to jazz up her look.

She remembers the moment vividly. Kate was stripped down to her undies while two older women threw Valentino jackets and pearls on Kate. "They made me look like 'a lady who lunched' from Greenwich, Connecticut." Kate spent all this money on things that felt nothing like her.

So when did Kate develop her true signature style? It was only when she went on the show *CBS This Morning* and saw one of the hosts. She was everything Kate wanted to be: classic, but with a really funky edge. "I remember her whole outfit. It was so funky... a flippy skirt with a fitted top, and *great* earrings." She asked the producers, "Who styles Renee?" She called that stylist immediately. She's been her stylist ever since, and Kate now has a style that truly feels like her own.

But you don't need a stylist to follow some of Kate's killer advice. Here's what to do to find your own style:

1. **Recognize that fashion does matter.** "I know some women feel it's unfair, but it's true. Fashion does matter. People are judging you on your appearance. We did a study at *Cosmo* that showed that in a job interview the decision *not* to hire [someone] is often made within the first five minutes. And

you can be sure that is about your look. It's simply not irrelevant." The first step is knowing that it's important.

2. **Figure out what makes you look good and feel good.** Kate's first recommendation for this? "I don't care if it's Instagram, or taking tear sheets out of a magazine. Start pulling out what fashion appeals to you." Try some things on and see what works for your body type. Keep going until you find something that you like, that's the shape that you need. Kate says to shop with a friend who will be honest with you and trust her, not the salesperson.

3. **Create a style philosophy.** Kate suggests that it can be helpful to find three words that describe your style. Similar to a company's mission statement—what three things would you say about your style. That way, "when you pick up that cool purple distressed leather miniskirt, and you ask yourself, is this classic, elegant, and refined, you'll know to put your wallet down. You have to commit to your three words and really, don't deviate."

4. **Last but not least, never underestimate the importance of shoes and bags.** "You might think people don't notice, but they do. They really do." A great bag says you mean business. And shoes should not only look good, they should make you feel good, too. "I remember at the *Cosmo* photo shoots, the design director would put the models or celebrities in stilettos. I'd say, But we don't photograph their feet. She'd say to me, Yes, but it makes them feel tall and powerful and in charge." Get the right shoes and the right bags to make you look and, more important, *feel* your best.

KATE'S TIPS

❋ What three words define your style? Write them down. Go
   through your wardrobe and ask yourself: Does all of my
   clothing fit within my three-word style limit? If not, and if it's
   a piece you don't love or don't wear, donate or toss it.

❋ Save photos of the styles you love and see which fit your shape
   best. Don't deviate from those; they will always make you
   look great.

CHAPTER 14

Figure Out Your Family Plan

WE SPEND ENORMOUS amounts of time planning our outfits—and we spend even more planning our careers. Career books sell through the roof; we attend job fairs and network at conferences, hire coaches, all of it. But when it comes to setting a life plan involving whom you choose for a life partner, or when to have kids—well, most of us expect that to happen organically. It doesn't help that there are not really as many options for educating yourself on how to make the best choices.

For me, I found that my best choice was made in choosing the right mate (albeit the second time around). I knew Dave would be a true partner in every capacity because beyond simply sharing values and common interests, he was—and still is—a fifty-fifty partner with me in all things.

Sometimes, this means my taking a backseat in roles that are typically reserved for moms. For instance, Dave is a frequent special guest in our children's classrooms. Teachers throughout Port Washington have received entertaining classroom sessions from "Multiplication Man," "Al G. Bro," and "Sergeant Simon Sez." When I show up to school for a standard "mystery reader" event, the kids often welcome me with a resounding "Ugh, where's Kate's dad?"

Generally, I find that picking someone who believes that you are equal partners helps you both achieve your career goals *and* your life goals. And together, you can answer one of the most important questions out there: when and if you want to have children.

I had three babies at three very different times in my life. In late 2002, I was sitting in my one-bedroom apartment that bordered the Long Island Railroad tracks, holding the positive pregnancy test in my hand. I was a top-selling salesperson, early in my career at twenty-five years old. I also knew that my (first) marriage was in deep trouble and that, more likely than not, I would be having this baby on my own. I took a breath and weighed my options, thought about the impact of having a child on my career and my life, and went for it. Charlotte was born in May 2003. I took six weeks of maternity leave. I leaned in, experienced success in my career, and loved being a mother—but boy, was it challenging.

In December 2006, I was newly remarried and had just left my full-time sales management job to start a consulting gig that would one day turn into Likeable Media. Feeling on top of my game, I was thrilled this time to see another positive pregnancy test. Kate was born in July 2007. At that time, I was consulting clients from home, watching *The View*, and slowing down, allowing my husband to step up and run the business, which he grew at light speed. Call it leaning out or taking a breather—whatever it was, it was pretty awesome. I came back to help take us over the finish line.

In late 2011, Likeable Media was a success, and I was at the top of my game professionally, but life felt incomplete. Dave and I decided we wanted another baby. Except this time, it wasn't as easy. Experiencing miscarriage after miscarriage, I was leading a company and looking like a huge success while inside, I was suffering greatly.

In 2014, after taking a long break from trying to have a baby, we gave it one last go. I was now thirty-eight, and financially secure. I became pregnant with my last baby, my miracle baby, and gave birth in April 2015. I took a whopping six months off, and returned to work with a full-time nanny in tow.

As I have had children at all different stages of my career, young women often ask me when is the right time in your career to have children. My answer?

Always and never. It's never easy to have them. It's always a good time because it's never a good time.

CARRIE'S TIPS

* There is no perfect time to have children.
* Your family plan is only somewhat in your control. You can't totally dictate the terms. But it's still worth putting effort and passion into planning your personal life, like you probably already do in your work life.

Raising Kids Is a Career in Itself

I interview a lot of brilliant career women in this book and on my podcast. But I also wanted to talk to one of my favorite women, proud stay-at-home mother for fifteen years Anita Rosner. Or, as she calls her job, the CEO of the Future Leaders Development Program.

Anita knew two things growing up: she wanted to have kids, and she wanted to be a stay-at-home mother. When she first got married, her husband said, "You know, if you don't want to work anymore, you don't have to." Well, that sounded great to a woman who had been working since she was fourteen years old.

Anita decided to stay at home and live a life of leisure. But within the first three weeks, it hit her. She may have made the wrong decision. "I had gone into a dark place when I started trying to make origami cranes out of my husband's underwear when folding the laundry," Anita says with a laugh. "I was a lady who lunches, but all of my friends were working, so I lunched alone."

After that, Anita went back to work for a private investor for a few years, until she got pregnant. She went to her boss with the news, ready to announce that she was going to retire so that she could be at home with her baby. His response: "But we're really baby friendly. We're going to give your baby its own office." And he did. Anita's baby had his very own office on Madison Avenue, complete with a crib and a playpen.

When Anita became pregnant with her daughter, she knew she couldn't bring two kids into the office. So she finally ended up becoming the stay-at-home mom she always wanted to be. The only problem came when she attended cocktail parties and barbecues, where people inevitably asked: "What do you do?" Anita would simply respond, "I'm a stay-at-home mom."

Every time, the conversation would come to a screeching halt.

"I'd have people literally walk away from me," Anita remembers. "Like there was nothing to talk about after that." So she decided that the next time someone asked her that question, she would reply: "I'm raising tomorrow's leaders." Because that's really what all mothers do.

As Anita explains to people, including her feminist daughter, who has strong opinions about the matter: "It's a woman's job to raise better people. So if you're going to be home raising your kids, that's the most important job you can have. Because you're helping shape the future."

Originally, Anita didn't question her decision to stay home with her kids. But when others did, she began to rethink her choices. She'd get angry at herself for doing so—she was proud of the work she was putting in with her family. She made a vow to not only use her "tomorrow's leaders" line in conversation, but to have enough confidence in her decision that she never wavered again at an awkward pause in the conversation.

When Anita's kids hit their late teenage years, she decided it was time for a career renaissance. Since she'd been off Wall Street for over fifteen years now, she felt hesitant getting back in the game. She decided to try something new . . . which was to dive headfirst into pursuing her passions.

She started with a comedy blog called *SNORK*, which turned into a comedy podcast, which turned into a full-fledged acting career. Anita now stars in Off-Broadway plays, music videos, and commercials. She doesn't regret the time at home for one second— in fact, she credits it with giving her the confidence to try acting. "I was literally starting over, so it was a chance to ignore all the voices in my head and follow the truest voice in my heart."

ANITA'S TIPS

❋ If you're a stay-at-home mom looking for a new title, call yourself a CEO of the Future Leaders Development Program. Because that's what you are and that's an incredibly important job to have.

❋ It's never too late to restart your career. What did you want to be when you were growing up? If you're not that yet, what's stopping you from trying it?

Get Creative and Make Your Career Work for You and Your Family, Not the Other Way Around

Unlike Anita, Lynne Jarman-Johnson, now CMO of Consumer's Credit Union, always had it in her DNA to work. She also wanted a big family. She had six kids over the course of ten years—all while building a very successful consulting career. She knew that a standard corporate job wouldn't work with that many children, so she invested in a home office and a great caregiver (well, many great caregivers over the years) and got to work.

Through it all, Lynne says, the lesson was to be honest with yourself and others about where you are at that moment in your life.

Lynne recalls a time just three weeks after her sixth child was born, when a new potential client called with an urgent request to meet. Lynne was on maternity leave at the time; she had given her caregiver time off, as she acclimated the newest baby, Ellie, into the family. Still, she knew she didn't want to disappoint the client.

"Okay," Lynne said, "I'll come meet with you, but you're also going to meet Ellie, my newest daughter."

Off Lynne went, wearing the most professional outfit that she could for a body that was reshaping itself, carrying Ellie in her car seat. Not only did she win the client, but she kept them for years.

Lynne recalls a young woman in the room who was early in her career and hadn't yet had children. Twenty-one years later the two are best friends and Lynne's heart swells when her friend recalls their first meeting: "You really changed my perspective during that meeting. You showed me that success is not always achieved in the corporate world—that success can be building the life you want on the terms you want." Lynne agrees. As long as you are honest with people, and they're okay with what's going on in your life, you can still be professional and succeed.

Looking back, Lynne has another memory of working her family plan in a way that all the kids now talk about around the dinner table as adults. Lynne and her husband, a trial attorney, always involved the kids in their work lives, too. Lynne recalls having her kids voice cartoon characters for brand mascots, as well as having them tutor her on social media when she needed to get savvy for brands. And before every big trial, her husband would sit the entire family down and practice his opening statements. These experiences not only got the kids interested in their parents' careers, they taught them that doing something you love is of the utmost importance.

LYNNE'S TIPS

❊ Be honest about your limitations as a working mother. People are more understanding than you think.

> ❋ Talk to your kids about your work. It will get them engaged in
> what you do and it will teach them to do what they love.

Perfection Is Overrated, Especially for Moms

I was at a fortieth birthday party of an uber-successful entrepreneur when I saw her across the room. There she was, Kass Lazerow, wife of Mike Lazerow and cofounder of Buddy Media, which had recently sold to Salesforce for $745 million. She and Mike were the ultimate power couple in my eyes. I also saw so much of who I wanted to be in Kass. Mike was the face of Buddy Media, the public figure. Kass? She was the operator, and she just seemed to get shit done. She didn't seem like most tech entrepreneurs to me. There was zero arrogance, and also, unlike most of the people in the tech bubble we were living in at the time, zero bullshit. I had never met her, and I knew I needed to.

When you approach someone who's had a tremendous success like Kass has, it's very challenging. I'm sure people come out of the woodwork once you "hit it big." My questions for Kass weren't about how to grow a multimillion-dollar empire, nor were they about investing in my company. My questions were about how the hell she managed to grow a behemoth of a company with her husband, while raising three children, and all coming out alive.

I followed up after that party with a request to get together, and Kass was all for it. A friendship was formed based on a commonality that most women don't share: what it's like to run a high-growth company with your husband while simultaneously running a rapidly growing family.

At our first lunch, I was going on and on about planning my

daughter Charlotte's bat mitzvah. The favors! The invites! I had to handpick everything, I told her. I was *exhausted*.

"Carrie," Kass said to me. "Want to hear the greatest advice I've ever gotten?"

Um, Kass Lazerow, my idol, wanted to tell me her greatest advice? "Okay, shoot," I tell her.

"No one gives an award for 'Most Tired Mom.'"

Kass started telling me that she used to do everything herself. Birthday party favors, school cupcakes, and more. But once she had the tired mom epiphany, she outsourced the little shit. She went on to say that this was not just for people who can afford "nannies and housekeepers and personal assistants."

Learning to outsource or forget the little stuff simply comes from letting go of the need to control everything and make it perfect. "I think it's like a switch goes off. You birth the baby, and you feel an immediate need to do all of the things associated with parenting—even when they're small menial tasks that someone else can do. As moms, we're all killing ourselves, and it's unnecessary. You can outsource, you can delegate, you can even skip some stuff, and still be a good mother," she said.

Kass has a theory that you can only be truly great at one thing at a time—and that "having it all" is only possible when you accept that you can't have it all at the exact same time. "When I was deep into Buddy Media's growth, my oldest son started showing signs of depression. I couldn't be great at all things at the same time. So I rotated. I got him every resource available while I pushed through the growth and eventual sale of Buddy, which I did and did well. The moment the transaction happened, I dedicated myself to being a full-time mother. I was always good at lots of things. But I can only be truly great at one thing at a time."

This resonated so much with me. I often feel like my life is a juggling act in a circus, and I'm juggling myself, my work, my relationship, and my children. At any moment, there's only one ball in my hand. The rest? I'm trying to project a semblance of confidence while praying the rest don't drop.

Throughout my years of knowing Kass, she's given me plenty of pearls of wisdom like this. These pearls include bits of everything, from wearing beanies in the winter so you look stylish without having to constantly blow out your hair, to tips on parenting, working with your husband, and more.

All of Kass's advice leads to one important theme for me—that is, to abandon the notion of perfection. Wearing a beanie allows you to have less than perfect hair. Outsourcing allows you to focus on improving the most important parts of your life. And accepting that you won't be great at everything allows you to be just a little less hard on yourself.

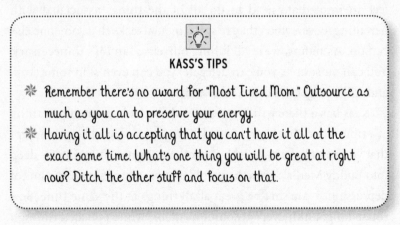

KASS'S TIPS

❋ Remember there's no award for "Most Tired Mom." Outsource as much as you can to preserve your energy.

❋ Having it all is accepting that you can't have it all at the exact same time. What's one thing you will be great at right now? Ditch the other stuff and focus on that.

Talk Early and Often about Your Family Plan

To bring this chapter home, it's time I turn to Allyson Downey. Allyson is the author of *Here's the Plan: Your Practical, Tactical Guide to Advancing Your Career During Pregnancy and Parenthood*. It's hard to imagine this brilliant, well-educated, strong woman experiencing pregnancy discrimination in the workplace, but that's exactly what happened to her. In fact, it was the catalyst for writing her book in the first place.

Allyson joined Credit Suisse after graduating from business school at Columbia. She was brought on board with an MBA class of about eighteen people at Credit Suisse. At the time, the five-year retention rate was horrific. Allyson became the shining star. A former political fundraiser, she was using her Rolodex to bring in wealthy clients for the bank, and her manager told her that "she was the best hope for this MBA class of recruits—that only a few from the class would make it through, and [he] was sure she would be one." It was right about that time, nearly ten months after joining Credit Suisse, that Allyson discovered she was pregnant. At thirteen weeks, she told the company about her pregnancy, making sure to convey early that she wanted to return after just six weeks.

Suddenly, Allyson was told by her doctor, she had pregnancy complications and needed to be on bed rest. Still fully determined to be working to her fullest, Allyson called work to fill in her manager and HR, and to find out what accommodations could be made so that she could work from home. What she received back shocked her.

Radio silence.

Allyson called and emailed every single day for two weeks. She called her manager. She called Human Resources. She called the managing director. She received zero response from anyone. Allyson was in a tailspin. The complications of the pregnancy were making her feel like her baby could die. The lack of communication from her company made her feel like she'd be fired. She was despondent.

Her doctor suggested copying her on the emails to HR, asking what type of documentation they would need from her obstetrician. Sure enough, that garnered a response. Allyson's manager did not respond, but HR did, giving her the number to call to go on disability.

Being pushed onto disability without ever having a conversation with her manager about transition, or who would handle her clients, was too much for Allyson. "It was a huge wake-up call. Even when you are tough as nails, a really hard worker, and a shining star, you can be completely sidelined by pregnancy." And for a long time, Allyson felt like a failure. Even though rationally she knew that the system had failed her, she felt like she failed— that she couldn't be a mother and be a success.

Eventually, Allyson left Credit Suisse and got a job at another company—one that paid better and was a better fit for her—and yet she felt much less confident. "I didn't feel like, as a mother, I could be a star. It had a lasting impact on me." Eventually, Allyson left to start her own business called weeSpring, which offered crowdsourced feedback on baby products for new moms. During that time, she was still in shock over what happened to her at Credit Suisse. When she surveyed over a thousand women in the weeSpring community, and one third said they had experienced some form of pregnancy discrimination, Allyson knew two things right away. First, she wasn't alone. Second, she needed to write a book to help women avoid this kind of discrimination in the future.

Allyson has two key points for women considering building their families while building their careers. The first point is to build your network. "After the Credit Suisse disaster, I had ten interviews lined up by the time my son was six weeks old. All of them were set up through my network." By building a strong network before you get pregnant, you can start to plan your next move if you experience anything remotely uncomfortable with your organization during your pregnancy.

The second tip is to communicate specifically about what you want around your maternity leave. Allyson speaks of a concept called "benevolent discrimination." "Sometimes employers think they're protecting you, when in fact they're discriminating against you. It is quite possible that my employer thought, 'Oh, Allyson will want to be on disability and not come back after such a complicated pregnancy.' The reality is, by not communicating clearly around what you want, you're letting them make that decision for you." Allyson did communicate—but perhaps not early enough. She recommends inserting the topic into conversation on more than one occasion. "Try saying something like, 'When I return from my six-week maternity leave, I won't want to travel for six months, but I'll be ready to return to work full-time.'" Figure out exactly what you want, and make sure to communicate it to your employer. "Like with most things," says Allyson, "communication is key." Allyson now spends much of her time communicating about the importance of developing your own post-maternity plans.

ALLYSON'S TIPS

❋ If your company is not supportive of new mothers, build a strong network outside of your job. They'll help you land somewhere if things don't work out with your current workplace.

❋ Talk early and often about your maternity plans so that your employer knows what you want and you can foster open and clear communication and expectations.

CHAPTER 15

Make Lemonade

WE'VE ALREADY DISCUSSED my love of Beyoncé, but have we discussed the work of art that is her album *Lemonade*? When *Lemonade* dropped without warning both in album and short film version, I devoured every second of it. What impressed me the most was how she took these deep pains—the (implied) infidelity by Jay Z, and the treatment of women of color throughout history, for instance—and turned the tables on it all. Beyoncé was literally making "lemonade" out of lemons, as the famous saying goes, and there's no doubt where the title of her album came from.

We spend so much time trying to achieve more, gain more, see more, do more, and we work hard to avoid the truth that there will also be times where significant events happen that make all of that nearly impossible. These moments in our lives are equally as defining as any major achievements we have, so it's essential to take a moment to explore how to deal with these inevitable challenges, as they are the ones that are the most likely to catch you off guard and change your plans and sometimes your whole life. In this chapter, you'll hear about some of these moments in the lives of women—moments that can take your breath away—and how these women, too, found a way to bounce back, and then some.

I call these women the "Lemonade Squad."

When it came to the start of my own Lemonade story, I couldn't understand it. I had done everything right. I was eating well, and exercising. I was taking my vitamins. I was not in a particularly stressful time in my life, and I had absolutely zero problems conceiving my first two children. But somehow, when Dave and I decided that we wanted a third baby—I ran into nothing but trouble.

I was convinced the first miscarriage was a fluke. *Oh, all women have them*, I thought to myself. This is no big deal. I felt funny that I even felt sadness. Running through my head: "You already have two children, and they're healthy. It's enough." But my heart was hurting.

Maybe I didn't deserve to have another baby. Maybe it was the universe's way of telling me that this was enough—I had my company, the kids, and Dave. This was a distraction I didn't need. Nevertheless, I pushed forward, and kept trying.

While I was sad after my first miscarriage, I was absolutely devastated after my second. The wind was completely knocked out of my sails and I had no idea how I would function. Still, I knew I had a family to take care of, and a company to run. Even though I wanted to stick my head in the sand and hide, I forced myself to move forward. Here's what I learned in the process:

■ **Be transparent and lean on your team.**
I didn't tell everyone at my company, Likeable Media, what I was going through, but I did tell my seven direct reports. I was very matter-of-fact and didn't ask for sympathy; I simply let

them know that I was struggling and needed help. And they stepped up big-time. When I couldn't spearhead and present a big client pitch, my team pulled it all together—and won the account. One of the major lessons I've learned in life is to never be afraid to ask for help. You'll be amazed at the result, and it will compel you to help others when you see that they need support as well.

- **Throw yourself in when you can, step out when you can't.**
In this case, I found that immersing myself in work really helped me get through. When it feels like your world has stopped dead in its tracks, sometimes the best solution is to move faster and harder. I focused on work and was productive. However, in 2010 when my father died, I stepped out instead. And the company was better for it. For me, either being fully in or fully out is the answer. Being in the middle leaves me distracted and more stressed.

- **Find a silver lining.**
If you believe that there is a positive reason for *everything* that happens in your life, the world seems a lot prettier. I have found it's a gift to have the ability to see the silver lining in all things— even a client screwup, delayed train, divorce, or worst of all, death. Choosing to embrace optimism makes you a better leader and a happier person. This doesn't mean that it's time to lose a grip on what's really happening; it just means that what's happening is here—today—and how you react to it is a choice. I opted to see my miscarriages as the universe saying that it wasn't time for me to have another baby—that it was time for me to focus on building Likeable. This helped me be more passionate in presentations to my team, and more focused on

working toward my goals. You can work through tough times if you see them as a gateway to greater times ahead.

P.S. The happy ending of this story? A few years later, Dave and I gave it one last go. Seth Franklin Kerpen was born in 2015.

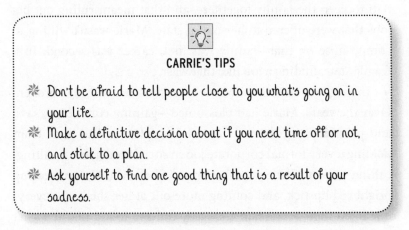

CARRIE'S TIPS

❋ Don't be afraid to tell people close to you what's going on in your life.

❋ Make a definitive decision about if you need time off or not, and stick to a plan.

❋ Ask yourself to find one good thing that is a result of your sadness.

Growing Apart Can Help You Grow Up

There is no better healing agent than time when you're dealing with a painful event. But sometimes, time is what caused the problem in the first place.

Marie Bonaccorse was married for ten years and had three children when it was clear that it was time for her marriage to end. "Just like your career is an evolution, marriages evolve, too. And one day, we woke up and we were two completely different people than when we started." Marie and her husband began the process of a very amicable divorce, but unfortunately, no matter how amicable, divorce is something that places your life in total upheaval.

The first step for Marie was mourning the loss of her marriage, which meant accepting that there was just "a totally new normal."

The second step was finding a job that could financially support her living on her own with her children. Marie had previously held senior positions at large companies, and she knew she could probably snag another similar position running social media for a brand. She also knew she wanted to stay close to home in Cincinnati to keep the family together—and that meant ruling out big jobs that were offered to her out of state. Marie wasn't willing to compromise on that—family was first, career was second. In a fragile state, finding a job like that wasn't so easy.

Throughout this time, Marie's ego was bruised and broken. Over the years, Marie had blossomed—gaining confidence, sass, and passion along the way. As an example, she had gone from holding a very formal corporate job in social media to consulting, calling herself "The Sassy Tweetress." She had taken to wearing bright red lipstick, and coming more out of her shell. Not everyone liked that. Marie had changed, and she found that it wasn't only her husband who didn't think the new Marie was right for him—some prospective employers didn't either.

"I was told I was too out there, too assertive," Marie said. "I was already feeling so low, and I was left playing the blame game—which I was already doing with the divorce. Every time I got a rejection, it fed that monster." Marie was questioning herself. She had finally really come into her own, and yet she felt rejected by everyone around her. It turns out, she just needed to recover from the pain and hurt of the divorce.

Ultimately, time was once again Marie's friend. Over time, she healed, and she found the perfect job for her personality—running social media at a new company. "They really *embraced* who I was. Strong, assertive, passionate, and a character. If I had compromised who I was, I might still be married, and I might have avoided a lot of pain. But I also wouldn't have found authentic joy."

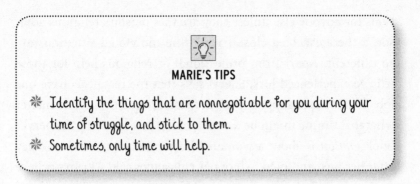

MARIE'S TIPS

❋ Identify the things that are nonnegotiable for you during your time of struggle, and stick to them.

❋ Sometimes, only time will help.

In the Face of Any Challenge, Choose Joy and Meaning

There's adversity, and there's unspeakable tragedy. Sheryl Sandberg, the chief operating officer of Facebook, first spoke about the loss of her beloved husband, Dave Goldberg, while addressing the 2016 graduating class of UC Berkeley. He died suddenly after suffering from a cardiac arrhythmia while on vacation in Mexico.

I watched Sheryl's speech, tears streaming down my face, and listened to this woman whom I had long admired talking about getting through the void—and about the lessons she learned from her husband's death. She said, "I learned about the depths of sadness and the brutality of loss. But I also learned that when life sucks you under, you can kick against the bottom, break the surface, and breathe again. I learned that in the face of the void—or in the face of any challenge—you can choose joy and meaning."

I wanted to talk more with Sheryl about this—and specifically, how she managed to get back to her new "normal"—and asked if she had any advice for women who have experienced a tremendous loss. When should they go back to work? What should they do to move forward? I felt like I had a million questions. In a way, there were a million answers. Everyone is different.

Sheryl was quick to say that no one should make recommendations for anyone else unless they are that person's religious advisor, a therapist, or a close friend. The individual situations are so different. Apart from professional or religious help for those who've experienced loss, Sheryl says that the rest of us have one job. That job is to support your decision around timing, no matter what that timing might be. For example, there is a story in Sheryl's book *Option B* about a woman who went back to work the day after her husband died. All of her colleagues said, "I can't believe you're here." The reality was, she did not want to be at home alone. She was absolutely devastated by her husband's death but she just wanted to do something, anything. And she chose to go to work. Sheryl says, "People did not help her by judging her for that. It did not mean that she didn't love her husband; it meant that she was dealing in the void, the best she could."

Other people will take a lot of time off. The best thing we can do, Sheryl says, is know that there is no right answer.

Sheryl credits her Jewish faith with helping her get through— turning to both her rabbi and her children's grief counselor. She took a total of ten days off—seven of which were for shiva, the intense period of mourning in the Jewish faith. The kids returned to school, and Sheryl returned to work. For her own family's experience, she felt like routine was important and helpful.

When I spoke to Sheryl, I asked about what she described as a "reservoir of sadness." How does one rise up from that, and specifically, how did you keep from being overcome at work? To address that, Sheryl thought back to the experience of her children's grief.

"My kids had arranged with school what we called 'cry breaks.' And they took them all the time. When they were overwhelmed, they could go to the guidance counselor, they could go outside with a friend, and for me, one of the lessons was that I had to let myself have those, too. When I tried to not have them, it was too hard. I found that when I went back to work, by the end of the day, I would just get in my car and bawl because it was all pent up from all day of trying to keep it together." While there is no one "right" way to experience grief, allowing yourself to feel it will leave you more open to eventually experiencing joy.

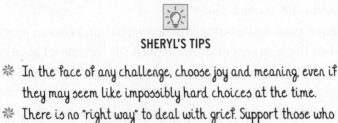

SHERYL'S TIPS

✳ In the face of any challenge, choose joy and meaning, even if they may seem like impossibly hard choices at the time.

✳ There is no "right way" to deal with grief. Support those who are grieving without judging how they choose to do so.

Heal Yourself by Helping Others Heal, Too

Sometimes, women who experience unimaginable loss end up changing their careers to help others with similar experiences.

Laura Winckel always loved quilts. But loving quilts and making them are entirely different things. As a teacher, Laura quilted mostly for fun and showed immense talent. Quilting also helped Laura get through unthinkable tragedy in her life. When her daughter, Sarah, died at age three from tuberous sclerosis, Laura's whole world stopped. "I thought I would never recover. I wanted only to be with Sarah. I remember taking a bottle of pills and wishing I'd never wake up."

Thankfully, Laura did wake up. Little by little, she tried to heal. "I am a person of great faith. I try very hard to look at Sarah's life and death as a blessing. It forced me to confront many things about myself that I was unable to see, and become a stronger, better person." Laura spent much of her time quilting, using it as a way to heal.

Years passed, when suddenly, Laura's mother, Lee, came into a large sum of money. Her first purchase? A long arm professional quilting machine for her daughter Laura. "My mother would loudly proclaim to anyone who saw her, 'You should see my daughter's quilts; she has such *talent!*'"

Laura's mom was admitted to the hospital, and Laura was with her when the long arm machine arrived. "I remember I got a call from a neighbor who said, 'Laura? There's a semi-truck in front of your house, darlin', no one can get by.'"

Turns out, a long arm quilting machine is huge. It took up Laura's whole living room. Every day, Laura would take pictures of the assembly of the long arm, and bring them to her mother. While at the hospital, it was decided that Laura's mom would need hospice care. Laura set it up in her home. She distinctly remembers wheeling her mother into her house. "The look on her face when she saw it—she was so proud."

Laura's mom died a few weeks later, and Laura decided that she was going to use this final gift from her mother as a way to help others get through their own grief.

Laura opened a quilting business, starting mostly with memory quilts. Made up of photos and old T-shirts, along with intricate quilting patterns, Laura's company, Quality Quilts by Laura, was born. Her business was burgeoning, attracting people from all over the country. For Laura, quilting is more than just a business. It's about healing and love. Laura would spend hours with each customer, listening to their stories and helping them heal.

"These precious quilts carry connections to our personal and cultural past. I love when a client comes into the studio, sees their quilt for the first time, and says, 'Oh yes, that's my grandma.'

Nothing connects us to our heritage quite like the cozy warmth and craftsmanship of the heirloom quilts passed from one generation to the next."

Looking back, Laura feels so proud that her career has been able to help others heal from loss.

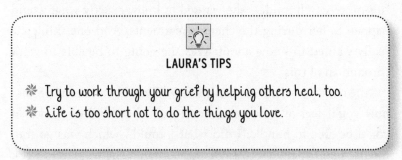

LAURA'S TIPS

❋ Try to work through your grief by helping others heal, too.
❋ Life is too short not to do the things you love.

Plan When You Can, and Lean on Your Ladies

It can feel impossible to deal with the kind of losses that Sheryl and Laura experienced. What about when it's not about surviving the loss of a loved one, but about your own survival?

Margit Detweiler is the founder of Gyrate Media, a content strategy firm that works with clients like GE and Verizon to develop their Web content. A Gen Xer, Margit was living a very busy life, not only running her firm, but also building up Tuenight.com, her popular Web site for women in her generation—the ones who are at the point in their lives where they are "not quite old, but not quite young."

All was going swimmingly, until one day her doctor discovered a cyst on one of her ovaries. Her doctor was not concerned, and performed minimally invasive surgery to remove the cyst.

When Margit got the call saying that there were cancerous cells on the cyst—that it was stage 2A, and that she'd need surgery and six months of chemotherapy—she was shocked.

"It's impossible to explain the feeling of utter panic and shock—you don't know who to call first, or what to do. It's this crazy new information that only you are sitting with, and you know it's going to change everything." Margit knew that the cancer was pretty early, and she was determined to beat it. She went into full-on research mode—she wanted to know exactly what would happen to her during the chemo treatments. And one thing she really wanted to know about: Was she going to be able to work through all of this?

The reality was, no one really knew. "Even doctors can't predict how you'll feel or how you'll react—or what kind of workload you'd be able to handle. I did what I could—which was go into intense planner mode." Margit was sure that she wanted to work through the next year. "I had heard from a lot of people that if you can keep working, even if you have to pare back, it's a good thing. Because when it's all over, reentry into 'normal life' can be very challenging."

Margit had about a month before her next surgery—and as a business person, she was determined to set herself up for success. For instance, a client had a project come up right when she was first diagnosed. As she was going through the diagnosis process, she was negotiating about how to structure the project. She assured them that she didn't have to be the face of the project, bringing on a colleague to help. She sought help from her editors and project managers, and used the time before chemo to be very logical in her approach—to prepare for the unknown.

Margit had made her plans. Now, it was time to start her treatment. A month after her diagnosis, she had her second surgery, and began her chemotherapy. For Margit, who had felt just fine before her diagnosis, it was like a wave of shock. Still, she was able to press on. But how?

By counting on amazing friends.

When Margit talked to me about this, she felt herself getting emotional. "I leaned on other women who really rose to the challenge. Being an almost fifty-year-old woman—those friendships I've built along the years, they came through in a big way." Women cooked, they offered to be guest editors on Tuenight.com, they simply came through in droves.

Another healing mechanism for Margit that helped get her through and also helped her professionally was writing. On Tuenight.com, Margit started a section called Ovarian Rhapsody, which chronicled her journey with cancer. In 2017, it was nominated for a coveted Webby Award for best personal blog.

Margit is a key part of my Lemonade Squad—because I watched her work through a tough cancer diagnosis and actually see it as a blessing. "This was a blessing to discover cancer cells on the cyst. I could have gone for years without discovering it was cancer, and it could have been too late. I thank that cyst all the time."

Another thing she's thankful for? The ability to use a terrifying diagnosis as a time to hit pause—a time to stop and reflect. "I did a lot of that and it gives you a whole other perspective you may not have had otherwise."

MARGIT'S TIPS

* If you have any time at all to plan before a life-changing diagnosis like this—do it. Planning helps you prepare for the worst, while still hoping for the best.
* Accept that you're going to need to rely on other people. Take the help from those who offer.

✳ Be kind to yourself. It's difficult to accept limitations from yourself when you're an accomplished person—but give yourself a break.

Sometimes Loss Can Be a Motivation for a Much-Needed Change

Sometimes, painful situations make you aware that it's not a career change that you need, but a life change.

Heather Wajer is currently the chief marketing officer for Whistle, which is the world leader in pet health and safety solutions. She's had an extensive career working for big brands like Livestrong, Baby Center, and many others. But before all of that, she had a very difficult start to her career.

Within months of Heather graduating from college, her mother was diagnosed with Lou Gehrig's disease. Heather moved in with her, became her caretaker, and started running the family business. Heather lived life as a complete caregiver for three years, suspending her career aspirations and running her mother's business out of necessity.

After her mother passed away, she felt completely lost. Her entire adult life had been dedicated to her mother's care.

"I had to take a long hard look at myself in the mirror and say, 'What do I want my life to be about?'" Heather says. Her mother was only fifty-one when she died, while she was smack in the middle of her own career. Heather knew that this was a key factor in how she'd live her own life going forward—she had to make every day count, and she needed to, above all else, live her life with passion. However, this was often easier said than done.

About ten years after her mother died, she was relatively happy with her career, and she'd started a family of her own. Still, she was numbing the pain of the loss of her mother in ways that were profoundly holding her back. Drinking, smoking, and tipping the scales at 315 pounds, Heather was finding it difficult to be a career woman and an active mother to her then three-year-old son. So, she made a friendly bet with a coworker to see who could lose forty pounds first. That turned into an entire lifestyle change. She started running triathlons, and eventually competed in her first Ironman.

This passion led to securing the ultimate passion job for Heather in 2012—vice president of marketing at Livestrong. Working through the loss of her mother, both literally and psychologically, has made Heather who she is today—a woman, 158 pounds lighter, nine years sober, in the career of her dreams.

HEATHER'S TIPS

❊ What single step can you take today to improve your own health? Try doing one small thing every day to do so.

❊ Don't develop unhealthy habits or addictions in order to numb the pain of a loss, or to make it go away. That will affect your career much more in the long run versus taking the time to grieve in a healthy way, even though it may hurt more at first.

CHAPTER 16

Win Like a Woman

WHILE WE ALL may not experience adversity in the same way, there's one thing we all have in common: we are women. (Unless you're one of our male supporters reading this book—in which case, yay you!) But being a woman in the workplace, and how much we experience that as an asset or a detriment, is entirely personal. For instance, I never knew that my leadership style was "girly" until I was knee-deep in research for this book.

With a company name like Likeable, you'd think we all sit around drinking Kool-Aid and singing "Kumbaya." That's not quite the case (though maybe we do let out a "kumbaya" every once in a while). Most of the time, though, as a leader, I have to make tough decisions, and those tough decisions have to be carried out.

When Dave and I used to work together at Radio Disney, he

used to call me MM. It stood for "master manipulator"—I know, you're thinking that sounds like a negative nickname, but in reality he meant that I could always get what I wanted, and deliver a message in a way where people still felt good. I was very diplomatic, and always very sweet, and I rarely had a confrontation.

Some might say that's great, but you know what? I was exhausted. I was so busy being indirect, and working angles to get what I needed, that it would take me way more time than if I simply said what I had wanted. I'd get caught up in a web of polite dodging and people pleasing. Everyone felt great . . . except me.

I didn't know that this leadership style was considered very female until I read a 2007 report from the Catalyst Group. In a study sponsored by IBM, titled "The Double-Bind Dilemma for Women in Leadership: Damned if You Do, Doomed if You Don't," the following conclusion was reached:

Women leaders are perceived as competent or liked, but rarely both. Respondents' comments revealed that when women behave in ways that are traditionally valued for men leaders (e.g., assertively), they are viewed as more competent. However, they are also perceived as not as effective interpersonally as women who adopt a more stereotypically feminine style.

Was it possible that I was getting what I wanted, but I was also perceived as ineffective? I only knew that the whole thing was exhausting me and I was tired, and it was all while I was still in the middle of reinventing the agency.

One of the areas around this reinvention was how we charged. I hate agency retainers and hourly rates; I always have. When I would receive an invoice from my lawyer, for instance, and he billed me $200 for 15 minutes to review and answer an email I sent (with a two-word reply), I would cringe. Turns out, I wasn't alone. Fortune 500 companies had entire groups focused on how to reinvent the agency model to save costs. I wanted to be ahead of the curve.

I invented something called the content credit system, where instead of paying by the hour, clients would pay by deliverable. I didn't charge them extra for email or phone-call time like typical agencies; I simply charged them by content piece and level of complexity.

My staff, including senior leadership, was pretty upset at the time by this decision. I heard it all: "Clients won't understand . . . they're used to the old way . . . we'll be fired . . . what if there are massive revisions and it impacts profitability . . . how do we explain it . . ." The list of complaints went on and on.

I had a choice. I knew exactly how I could finesse the situation and educate my entire team taking the same lovely flowery route I normally did. I could answer every question they had diplomatically, tapping into each of their needs to feel heard. Or, I could just lay down the law.

Maybe it was a result of reading that article, or maybe it was that I was finally stretched too thin and was too exhausted to gently woo them over to my side. But for the first time in my tenure as CEO of Likeable, I gave it to them straight.

"We are doing this. It's on you to figure it out."

And guess what? They appreciated it. So much so that they still talk about it years later. For me, occasionally dropping my "lady style" and acting with more male characteristics serves me well. And I find that using a blend of the two styles tends to make me both respected *and* liked.

> ### 🔆 CARRIE'S TIPS
>
> ❊ Being direct saves time and is ultimately more likeable. What are you dancing around that you need to say? Go say it, and say it straight.
>
> ❊ What key decision would you make today if you weren't worried about looking like a "bitch"? Try making it.

The Power of Being Assertive without Being Aggressive

So what about when your entire field is male dominated? Just ask Nisha Lulla, the associate vice president of hospital operations at Rush University Medical Center. Nisha was in supply chain management, which is an extremely male field, especially in the healthcare industry. Nisha had three things that made her different from the attendees at 95 percent of the meetings she attended once she entered senior leadership. First, she was a woman. Second, she was a woman of color. And third? Nisha was just thirty years old when she worked her way up into a senior position in supply chain management. On more than one occasion, Nisha recalls, she was mistaken for the assistant. Ten years ago the field was even less diverse than it is today, and it was hard for Nisha to feel like she was taken seriously.

It was because of this that Nisha felt she had to work much harder to overcome some of the perceptions . . . and that included, yes, trying to hide challenges associated with building your career as a woman—challenges that no man faces . . . like pregnancy.

In 2011, Nisha became the director of supply chain at the hospital, and at the time they were in the middle of building a new bed tower. The project cost $650 million. In addition to making sure all supplies and materials were seamlessly moved from the old building to the new, there was also a new technology to manage all of the materials. "Picture a project where you were literally having to ensure that operating rooms were moved perfectly and nothing was touched. *Not* a small project."

Nisha had worked on the project in her previous role, but now she was responsible for making sure that everything happened on schedule, and on budget. All of this in addition to actually managing the team that was getting it done.

The actual move to the new building took place over a weekend in early 2012. Nisha also happened to be twelve weeks pregnant at the time—and no one at Rush knew. She was horribly nauseated and remembers going to leadership and staff meetings and having to step out for a few minutes "to throw up in the bathroom and come back."

Nisha remembers, "The weekend of the move was crazy and of course not everything went exactly as planned. I could have told my team when to be there, what to do, and admonished them when things didn't go as planned, while I stayed home since I felt miserable. But instead I showed up each day before everyone and helped move supplies and equipment and made sure that everyone's issues were addressed. We moved over two hundred patients that weekend into the new hospital."

Nisha never wanted anyone to see her at a disadvantage because she was a woman. And pregnancy is not the only thing that can hold women back in a business setting. There's the quintessential dilemma of "when you're a man and you're assertive you are powerful. When you're a woman and you're assertive, you can be seen as a bitch."

Nisha's philosophy around that dilemma is to use the "iron hand in a velvet glove" method. "I like to think that I can go toe-to-toe with any man now. But my delivery is different. I'm assertive, but not aggressive. To be taken seriously as a woman, you have to take a different approach. That approach involves a lot of listening. When I listen to my team, I'm better able to support and guide them— even if I disagree."

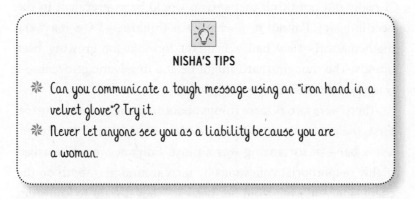

NISHA'S TIPS

❋ Can you communicate a tough message using an "iron hand in a velvet glove"? Try it.

❋ Never let anyone see you as a liability because you are a woman.

Focus on Great Results

Edlynne Laryea really didn't believe that sexism was a thing anymore. When she graduated from college with a degree in business with a focus on marketing, strategy, and IT, her class was split fifty-fifty in terms of gender. They were all setting out into the world together on an equal footing, or so she thought. In her industry, that was wishful thinking.

Soon after graduation, she got a job as a strategy consultant. As one of the only women in the room, she remembered a team meeting where they talked about how amazing it was that everyone could grow at the organization. "You can all be partners here one day," said the head partner. He looked around the room. "John, and Jason, and Thomas, and Rob, and Steve . . ." The pause before the next part felt deafening to Edlynne. "And even Edlynne." The room was filled with smirks and an uncomfortable silence. Even Edlynne? It became clear that there wasn't a natural path for Edlynne to make partner at that firm. Though she didn't react in the room, she knew that she would not stay at the company for very long.

Later on in her career, as a group brand manager for a well-known beer company, Edlynne was faced with sexism yet again. "I really did not think that sexism would be as prevalent in the beer industry. I'm not sure what I was thinking—I saw it as very mathematical—they had a brilliant formula for growing beer brands. The thought that I might be at a disadvantage because I was a woman didn't enter my mind."

There were two bizarre things about working in this industry. First, the environment was very social—your "client" was generally a bar—so socializing was a must. Edlynne would be asked highly inappropriate questions by men around her—both on the client side, and even from her bosses. "They'd want to know details about my relationships and my preferences. It was straight out of the 1950s." More often than not, she was mistaken for one of the "beer girls," the promotions staff who would wear skimpy outfits and sample beer. "Your outfit's over there, honey," the bartenders would say, assuming she was part of the hired team. They always reacted with surprise that she was there in a management capacity.

Now working in tech as the global director of digital partnerships for Johnson & Johnson (Consumer Products), Edlynne finds that she continues to be underestimated in some cases. In particular, when working with tech platforms. "Founders are often young and male, and they become perplexed when I ask specific and detailed questions about how the product works. It's like the back end is reserved for the backroom boys' club."

Edlynne also shares my understanding of the loud male social media agency owners. Edlynne remembers once showing a prominent male agency founder what she did on the Listerine brand and he looked at her simply amazed. As she recalls, "He asked, 'Where did you learn to *do* that?' The implication was that I had to have been taught by someone else to get the results that I did."

So, there are really two options here, when you're faced with the challenges that Edlynne has seen in her career. You can either walk around with a chip on your shoulder, or work it to your advantage. Edlynne chooses the latter. "I find that one of my single greatest advantages is being underestimated. It's like expectations are lower and therefore people are astounded by the work and the results. I used to get mad, and now I use that energy to push me further, faster. I show great results and impress them—and I'm never underestimated again."

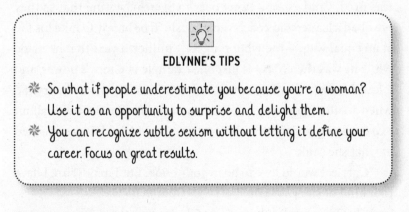

EDLYNNE'S TIPS

❋ So what if people underestimate you because you're a woman? Use it as an opportunity to surprise and delight them.

❋ You can recognize subtle sexism without letting it define your career. Focus on great results.

Speak Up and Speak Out!

As an agency CEO, there was no question about who I'd have close out this section on dealing with how women are treated in the workplace. Cindy Gallop has a long history of working at and running advertising agencies—her last position at one was when she was the chairman and president of BBH New York, a large creative agency. For five years straight, I have watched Cindy keynote the 3Percent Conference, a conference dedicated to changing the gender ratio in the advertising world. (At the time of the conference's inception, just 3 percent of creative directors at advertising agencies were female.)

I became obsessed with Cindy's badassery. She was strong and powerful; she used very direct, sometimes profane language to express her thoughts . . . and when she expressed them, people listened. There was that time that Saatchi & Saatchi chairman Kevin Roberts declared that gender bias in the ad world "is fucking over" and attacked Cindy for "making things up" in a Business Insider interview. Cindy's reply was to ask the ad industry to respond to him on Twitter, and her forty-six thousand followers, many of whom were prominent leaders in the industry, did. After Kevin was fired, Cindy shot a tweet over to Saatchi, stating that as they now had a leadership coach vacancy, she'd be happy to take his job at an equal wage—the whopping $4.1 million a year that he made while he was there. This is just one example of Cindy's power, and I loved how brazenly she called out sexism in the industry. So when I called her up to ask for an anecdote for the book about experiencing sexism when she was in the ad world, I was shocked at what she said.

"Carrie, I would love to be in your book. But I'm not sure I have that kind of story for you."

What? Cindy, the champion of destroying the rampant sexism that runs through the ad world, did not experience sexism as she rose up the ranks at some of the biggest agencies in the world?

Turns out, that's not exactly right either. You see, Cindy's theory is that "fish don't know what water is." In other words, when you are immersed in something, it's difficult to see it for what it is.

So, while it was likely that she experienced sexism constantly, it was simply just the way it was. She never took the time to think about it because she was too focused on doing amazing work.

For many years, Cindy was the token female at conferences, representing her agency. She would sit on a panel or run a keynote, talking about what constitutes great creative, or how she launched a big campaign, always with the goal of driving business back to the agency where she worked. She always had to be very careful not to offend clients, or her agency . . . so the mouthy, fierce woman I knew had to speak in front of an audience and bite her tongue.

In 2005, Cindy left her job and started to consult. And from that point on, any tongue biting was not done on a conference stage at all. Cindy gave her first talk as an entrepreneur at a digital summit. Now, instead of being inside of a large organization, she was able to see the advertising world from the outside. And what she saw made her angry.

Cindy started speaking about the realities of the advertising industry, about the pay gap between men and women and the underrepresentation of people of color. Kat Gordon saw her speech and asked her to keynote the first 3Percent Conference.

"When I give my talks, many women have similar experiences to mine—they're fish in water. But when I speak, it's like a lightbulb goes off within them, and they realize what's happening around them. Once their eyes are open, they're able to start to effect change from within."

Cindy's talks resonated so much that she keynoted the next four 3Percent Conferences, delivering a different message each time. And her message and Kat Gordon's 3Percent movement seem to be working, slowly but surely. The number of female creative directors has crept up to 11 percent. Cindy's goal? "The push for fifty-fifty gender balance for employment, at all levels and within all departments—if not more female than male, since it's been the other way around for far too long."

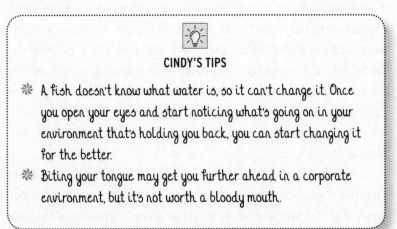

CINDY'S TIPS

❋ A fish doesn't know what water is, so it can't change it. Once you open your eyes and start noticing what's going on in your environment that's holding you back, you can start changing it for the better.

❋ Biting your tongue may get you further ahead in a corporate environment, but it's not worth a bloody mouth.

HATERS GONNA HATE—PROVE THEM WRONG: A CASE STUDY WITH KELLY COOK, CMO OF KMART

If I told you that the CMO of Kmart's nickname was Runway Roadkill, would you believe me? It turns out that before this brilliant marketer made it to the C-suite of a Fortune 500, she was a runway model who fell in front of a huge audience.

Right after high school, while attending college, Kelly set out to be a runway model. She remembers her first runway show like it was yesterday. "I was wearing a leather skirt, high heels, a denim jacket, and teased Tina Turner–like hair. 'Glamorous Life' by Sheila E.

was playing . . . I'll never forget that part." Kelly felt like she was about to throw up as she stepped out onto the stairs down to the runway.

Suddenly . . . SPLAT.

Kelly fell. In front of the entire audience. Immediately, she stood up, smiled, and acted like it was part of the show. Kelly sees this career start as the metaphor for her entire life. "I knew I was going to make mistakes my entire life. The question was, how was I going to handle them? Would I let it define me? Or would I get back up?"

Kelly feels that your true character is shown in those moments, and in leadership—handling mistakes with grace makes you a better leader. People relate to you, and feel more comfortable. True to form, Kelly embraced her mistake, and has maintained the nickname Runway Roadkill for her entire adult life—it is currently all of her handle names on social media.

Post–runway model disaster, Kelly set her sights on working in corporate at her hometown airline—Continental. There was just one holdup—Kelly quit college in her senior year, when she got pregnant with her first child. Continental refused to hire her—she had no experience, and had not completed her formal education. This made Kelly mad, but it also made her determined. She was going to prove herself to Continental Airlines if it was the last thing she did.

There was one way that Kelly could get a foot in the door—by joining the temp pool for secretaries and administrative assistants. Eventually, Kelly spotted a temp job as a financial analyst. A math major in college, Kelly was thrilled to take the temporary position. From day one, she fell in love. When the permanent position opened, she went to the hiring manager and said, "I am getting this job." The hiring manager took one look at her and said absolutely not. Again, she had limited experience and no degree—she was not a viable candidate for the full-time role. Kelly only had one thought at this point.

"I'll show you."

Kelly temped in the position for twenty-nine days, working as hard as she could. On day thirty, she accepted the permanent position as financial analyst at Continental Airlines. "Don't ever let anyone tell you you can't do something," says Kelly.

Kelly stayed with Continental for eleven years, growing into marketing and global customer engagement roles. Kelly was recruited to go to Waste Management, for a vice president position. Even though her lack of an undergraduate degree no longer seemed to be a factor for companies, it was bothering Kelly. She approached Waste Management about tuition reimbursement to complete her undergraduate degree. They had a better idea. An executive MBA program was opening at Tulane, and they were looking for executives to participate. Waste Management had researched it—if Kelly scored high enough on her GMATs, she could get in without the undergraduate degree. Thrilled, Kelly activated her "I'll prove it to you" philosophy and studied furiously for the GMAT. She was admitted to the MBA program with a focus on finance, and ended up receiving not one but two master's degrees—all without ever completing her undergraduate education.

When Kelly received an opportunity to work at DSW Shoes, she really didn't think twice. Because, well, SHOES. Over the course of six years, Kelly worked her way up to become the chief marketing officer. In learning about the team beneath her, Kelly discovered that they had a real fear of failure, which was holding them back from taking risks.

Kelly set out to make it okay for people to have enough confidence to make mistakes. She founded the CLM Awards at DSW—which stood for "Career Limiting Moves." People would submit and document their mistakes, and they'd get added to a running list. At the end-of-year holiday party, Kelly would host an awards ceremony, where she'd select the top 10 mistakes to be featured. They'd all receive gift cards, and the winner would receive "the ugliest shoe I could find as a trophy!" Mistakes ranged from sending an incorrect coupon offering 100 percent off to a list of five million people to embarrassing the CEO in a meeting. When enough time had passed, everyone was able to laugh about it. "I had to teach them to take risks. Two times out of ten you're GOING to fall flat on your face. But what about the other eight times? If you never take chances you don't get those eight. You get zero."

Kelly has worked through several challenges in her career by focusing on her confidence. "After all," she says, "confidence is going after Moby Dick in a rowboat, and bringing the tartar sauce with you."

CONCLUSION

The Secret to Working It Revealed— WORK IT THE WAY YOU PLEASE

THIS BOOK HAS been as much of a journey for me as it was for you. I've learned more from these women than I ever could have hoped and I hope you have, too. Journeys are like that—you never know exactly what you're going to pick up along the path until you start traveling it. I'm going to leave you with one of my favorite journeys—a story that touches on a little bit of every theme we've talked about here.

Back in college, I was looking at a variety of internships. When my dad mentioned that his court reporter was the mother of a top executive at one of the world's largest advertising agencies, I was so excited I could hardly breathe. I had long fantasized about an agency career that was similar to Heather Locklear's on the hit '90s television show *Melrose Place*. Well, this was my *Melrose Place* moment come true. It turns out not only was the court reporter's daughter a top media buyer there, but her daughter was married to a VP in account services, and they both had agreed to give me an informational interview for an internship. I put on my best red suit and walked into the office, ready to accept whatever grunt work they'd give me just to get in the door.

The power couple each interviewed me separately, and mainly they wanted to know the same thing—what area of advertising did I want to work in? Media buying was very different from account services, which was very different from copy or design . . . what interested me? I gave my very best Miss America answer: "Well, I'm just happy to be here and learn."

Wrong answer.

Both Mr. and Mrs. Melrose Place basically told me the same thing—you're a great kid and come back when you have focus.

I left feeling completely dejected. I had made an idiot of myself in front of very important people. How could I be so wishy-washy? I should have just picked an area, even if I wasn't sure. I kept replaying the interviews in my mind, over and over . . . cringing at my own naiveté.

It ended up being a good thing, of course, since I landed at Radio Disney and that launched my whole career. But throughout my career, at different points, I thought about that interview, and remembered one of the most important lessons that I ever learned: Focus is essential.

And I have used that lesson. I focused on growing as a salesperson. I focused on finding the right partner and ensuring he got the wedding he wanted and deserved. I focused on creating a career that allowed me to raise my children and spend the time I needed with them. And when times got tough, I focused my company's services in order to allow it to grow. And in that process I grew a lot, too.

You can imagine the irony when just twenty years later, my assistant told me that the top executives at that very same agency wanted to meet with me. I literally had no idea as to why. Were they looking at a list of failed internship candidates to see who they missed out on twenty years later? Hardly. It turns out, they were looking for companies to acquire, and wanted to check out Likeable.

As I sat in front of the Global CEO and CFO, telling them how I had productized my business, with an offering that turned agency compensation on its head—how I took the company from unprofitable to above-average margins, and how I was nimble enough as a small social-first shop to win the social business of the big-name clients they so desperately wanted to serve—I knew it had all come full circle. I told them about the podcast, and my strategy of winning with women decision makers. I watched their eyes light up as I told them my road map . . . and suddenly I knew myself. That I had meandered through my career, feeling like I had no confidence, when in reality I knew exactly what to do and when. It was all within me, and here I was, sitting with the very organization that represented the epitome of my inner struggle. Unlike my internship interview, I *owned* this room. It was mine for the taking, and I enjoyed playing the verbal game of ping-pong that showed why and how our small agency would be so desirable to an organization like theirs.

And we were. We were desirable to them, and to several other potential acquirers who have come in and out of these doors. And it's funny, I used to dream of being acquired—of that big payday that I've worked so hard for. The day that I could throw my beret up in the air, just like Mary Tyler Moore, and say, "You're gonna make it after all." But the reality is that in the process of talking to hundreds of women, I've learned that the brass ring isn't always the seven-figure check that changes your life. Sometimes it's about building a business, and really a life, on your own terms—and working it the way you best see fit.

There is no one right answer. There is only your answer.

Thanks for taking this journey with me. Now go work it the way you want.

EXERCISE FIVE

The Secrets for Success

Well, we've come to the end of our journey together. If you're like me, your head is full of these incredible stories, and you've got a lot on your mind.

I want you to stop right now and take a minute to take three deep breaths. Do it right now! (Look, even if you think I'm full of it, it still can't hurt to take deep breaths, so do it!) Close your eyes, and think back to what you wanted to get out of this book—be it inspiration, or encouragement, or maybe just entertainment.

Chances are, some of these stories are stuck in your head. But I don't just want you to remember them—I want you to act on them. So let's think about what we've learned, and what actions we can take to use these stories to better WORK IT in our own lives.

I was inspired by:
(name your favorite WORK IT Women)

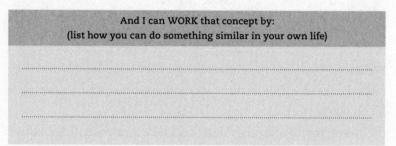

The lesson was:
(write down what you got out of the story)

....

....

....

And I can WORK that concept by:
(list how you can do something similar in your own life)

....

....

....

Awesome. Good luck, girl, and go WORK IT.

Acknowledgments

This was never supposed to be a book. This was supposed to be a collection of podcast interviews about social media, as told by women who work in the industry. It only became a book because I was encouraged to channel my confidence and make it so—because of the cheerleaders in my corner. These acknowledgments call out just a few of those cheerleaders—for whom I am immensely grateful.

First and foremost, Dave, I have to thank you for so many things—but in this context I'll thank you for reminding me about the book I really wanted to write, for gently nudging me to pitch it, and for advising me throughout the entire process. I've watched you do this for others many times, but I never realized how amazing you were at it until you did it for me. You are my partner in all things, and I'm so glad to be #inittogether with you.

Theresa Braun, this book never would have happened if you hadn't first compiled the hundreds of hours of podcasts into a collection of stories. Even though we ended up going in a different direction, your words gave me the confidence to move forward. You inspire me as a writer and as a friend.

My agents, John Maas and Celeste Fine—you are champions. Celeste, I remember when you told me that the *Social Ladies* book was not my book—that there was a bigger story to be told. You were right. And John, you were the perfect person to have in my corner.

Candie Harris, I am 100 percent positive that I would have self-combusted during this whole process without your incredible guidance, mentorship, and love. You are one of the most important people in my life, and your legacy is cemented in this book. I hope the snippets of your wisdom found throughout these pages resonate with others the way they have resonated with me and the entire Likeable family. You are a gift and a treasure.

Jo Hague, you handled every single interview request with ease, you kept me on track, and you never once complained when I begged you to bring me Dunks. You are the best assistant a girl could ask for.

Rachel Hadley, you not only kept Likeable Media afloat during my time spent on this book, you made it even better. I am so grateful to you and the Likeable team. Special shout-out to Gillian Stippa and Chris Barr for photographing the cover, to Jessi Chang for the incredible artwork, to Michelle Greenbaum for her tweet skills, and to Valerie Tirella for understanding my creative vision. And of course all of my fabulous cover ladies—Jaime x 2, Honey Comer, Jenn Burgess, Michelle Rivas, and Bea Arthur (an honorary Likeable employee!).

Mom, aka Da, you made the book so much better—both from your killer editing skills, and your insight. Thanks for making sure I didn't sound like an idiot.

So many incredible friends helped me through this process, which was entirely new to me. Special thanks to Emily Baxter for the endless texting sessions that provided necessary distractions; to Beth Ain for her incredible insight as an author, former editor, and dear friend; and to Marlene and Dale, who gladly read sections without complaining at all. Thanks to the ladies of TheLi.st for providing constant support, connections, and love!

Miss Stephanie Bowen—you are one incredible editor. You are thoughtful in your approach, and you are so dedicated to your craft—it is so abundantly clear to me that you love what you do. I see a lot of myself in you, and I look forward to watching you soar in your career and your life. Amanda Shih, thanks for being the best pinch hitter I could have asked for. Margaret and the Cave Henricks team, thanks for bringing this home with me!

To Kate, Charlotte, and Seth: Kate, thanks for showing me what true confidence really is. Char, thanks for not having too much teenage angst during the writing of this book. Seth, thanks for making me smile throughout the process with your never-ending supply of cuteness.

And finally, to every woman featured in this book—your insight, your wisdom, your humor, your candor—it is a gift to me, and to all of our readers. Thank you.

About the Author

photo by Diana Berrent Photography

CARRIE KERPEN is the CEO of Likeable Media, an entrepreneur, podcaster, writer, and sought-after speaker. Best known for her work growing Likeable Media from a two-person husband-and-wife team to a global social media agency, Carrie is also the host of the *All the Social Ladies* podcast. She has interviewed over two hundred women throughout the course of her career, and her writing has appeared in *Inc.*, *Forbes*, and *Fast Company*, among others.

Carrie lives in Port Washington, New York, with her husband, Dave, and her three children, Charlotte, Kate, and Seth.

Carrie taught you to WORK IT.

We help brands do the same.

Contact info@likeable.com for
a complimentary evaluation of
your brand's social media content.

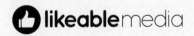